CONGRESS
AND THE
SEPARATION OF POWERS

CONGRESS AND THE SEPARATION OF POWERS

by
John L. FitzGerald

PRAEGER

PRAEGER SPECIAL STUDIES • PRAEGER SCIENTIFIC

New York • Philadelphia • Eastbourne, UK
Toronto • Hong Kong • Tokyo • Sydney

Library of Congress Cataloging-in-Publication Data

FitzGerald, John L.
  Congress and the separation of powers.

  Includes index.
  1. Separation of powers—United States.
  2. Delegation of powers—United States.
  3. Administrative procedure—United States.
  4. Legislative power—United States. I. Title.
  KF4565.F58   1985   342.73'044   85-12187
  ISBN 0-03-004634-3 (alk. paper) 347.30244

Published in 1986 by Praeger Publishers
CBS Educational and Professional Publishing, a Division of CBS Inc.
521 Fifth Avenue, New York, NY 10175 USA

© 1986 by Praeger Publishers

6789 052 987654321

Printed in the United States of America on acid-free paper

INTERNATIONAL OFFICES

Orders from outside the United States should be sent to the appropriate address listed below. Orders from areas not listed below should be placed through CBS International Publishing, 383 Madison Ave., New York, NY 10175 USA

Australia, New Zealand
Holt Saunders, Pty, Ltd., 9 Waltham St., Artarmon, N.S.W. 2064, Sydney, Australia

Canada
Holt, Rinehart & Winston of Canada, 55 Horner Ave., Toronto, Ontario, Canada M8Z 4X6

Europe, the Middle East, & Africa
Holt Saunders, Ltd., 1 St. Anne's Road, Eastbourne, East Sussex, England BN21 3UN

Japan
Holt Saunders, Ltd., Ichibancho Central Building, 22-1 Ichibancho, 3rd Floor, Chiyodaku, Tokyo, Japan

Hong Kong, Southeast Asia
Holt Saunders Asia, Ltd., 10 Fl, Intercontinental Plaza, 94 Granville Road, Tsim Sha Tsui East, Kowloon, Hong Kong

Manuscript submissions should be sent to the Editorial Director, Praeger Publishers, 521 Fifth Avenue, New York, NY 10175 USA

*To Genevieve Warren FitzGerald,
ever a source of unfailing support,
who read the manuscript and
made constructive suggestions in
the interest of clarity.*

ACKNOWLEDGEMENTS

I wish to acknowledge and express my sincere appreciation for the assistance provided by Relm Foundation, Inc., Ann Arbor, Michigan, whose financial support made this study possible. I am slso indebted to the School of Law of Southern Methodist University for making available secretarial, word processing and other assistance that facilitated completion of the study.

I am indebted to Joanne Lankford FitzGerald and Lieut. Col. John Warren FitzGerald for the extensive reasearch, organization and drafting of the text and notes for Chapter 3. I gratefully acknowledge the research and drafting services performed by Matthew Malloy FitzGerald with respect to Section D of Chapter 2 involving the National Labor Relations Board. The contributions of Professor Emeritus Roy R. Ray of the School of Law of Southern Methodist University and Geoffrey A. FitzGerald, Esq., Adjunct Professor of Law, Baylor University, are acknowledged in reviewing the manuscript and making suggestions that have improved the form and style of both text and notes.

I also express appreciation to the following persons who reviewed portions of manuscript drafts (appearing in parentheses below) and made suggestions for their improvement: Dee Pincock, former Assistant General Counsel, and Horace Slone, engineering assistant to a former commissioner of the Federal Communications Commission (Section A of Chapter 2); Federick Kirgis, Esq., former Chairman of the Administrative Law Section, American Bar Association (Section B of Chapter 2); Professor Emeritus Richard Sullivan of Boston College Law School, and Milton Denbo, Esq., former member of the Council of the Administrative Law Section (section D of Chapter 2); Adolph H. Zwerner, former Director of the Division of Law, Housing and Home Finance Agency (Section E of Chapter 2); Charles Hallam, former Librarian of the Supreme Court of the United States (with respect to source material in Chapter 3); and the late Professor Emeritus Arthur L. Harding of the School of Law of Southern Methodist University (Chapter 4).

CONTENTS

Chapter 1

INTRODUCTION

The U.S. Constitution requires that legislative, judicial, and administrative powers of the federal government be kept basically separate. This requirement is based on the flat statement in Article I that

> All legislative powers herein granted shall be vested in a Congress of the United States . . .

and the provision of Article II that

> The executive power shall be vested in a President of the United States . . .

and the provisions of Article III that

> Section 1. The judicial power of the United States, shall be vested in one Supreme Court, and in such inferior courts as the Congress may from time to time ordain and establish.

> Section 2 [Clause 1]. The judicial power shall extend to all cases . . . arising under this Constitution, the Laws of the United States, and Treaties made [and] to Controversies. . . .

Nevertheless, since the 1930s there has been an increasing tendency on the part of Congress to delegate discretion to administrative agencies. The statutes granting such authority are enacted in such broad and generalized form that they seem to constitute delegations of the "legislative powers" granted to Congress by Article I of the Constitution.

After the enactment of the Great Society legislation of President Lyndon B. Johnson, congressional sponsors stated that passage of the bills had been so hurried that a good deal of legislative amendment and revision would be required in the next session of Congress. It is questionable that much of this was undertaken or completed.

Most broad statutory provisions have their origins in legislative proposals transmitted to Congress by administering officials who have sought the utmost flexibility of action.

The Federal Trade Commission is empowered to prevent persons from using unfair methods of competition.[1] A state-approved plan for air pollution must comply with the "regulations and criteria" promulgated by the administrator of the Environmental Protection Agency.[2] Grants of federal funds are made available for "viable urban communities."[3] Heads of federal departments must purchase for public use American-made articles rather than articles of foreign manufacture unless they determine that this would be "... inconsistent with the public interest...."[4] Further instances of legislative provision of ill-defined authority to the Executive are available upon turning the pages of the U.S. Code.

Aware of the increased trend toward congressional transfer of apparent legislative powers to the Executive, the American Bar Association adopted a resolution in 1973. This resolution, reprinted in Appendix I, called upon the President of the United States, when he proposed a delegation of power to the Executive, to be specific, and urged Congress to enact no statute delegating power to the Executive unless it set forth definite standards for administrative action.

The trend of broad delegations of power, however, has continued unabated, and with it the threat of injury to the individual citizen by orders and regulations of administrators exercising legislative powers, though they are not elected officials.

A delegated authority frequently found in the statutes is the administrative power to make determinations in "the public interest," a term that, unless otherwise defined, must mean something on the order of "the general welfare." As an expression of legislative policy, the term is completely indefinite.

Is it desirable for Congress to enact a delegation along lines as broad as the following:

The Federal Communications Commission is authorized to regulate in the public interest national network organizations that contract to supply radio or television licensees with programs for broadcast, and may adopt rules and regulations to effectuate this purpose.

Or should the statutory authority thus delegated be spelled out with greater definiteness? Should the legislative policy be more sharply defined to describe the who, what, when, where, and how that together express the "public interest" objective in the mind of Congress? And is this practicable? (The delegation language in the example is hypothetical, but not uncharacteristic.)

How do the federal administrators deal with these grants of legislative authority? Chapter 2 offers an explanation in a brief survey of problems encountered by six administrative agencies that Congress has endowed with broad powers.

Are such grants of legislative power constitutional? This is the subject matter of Chapter 3, which discusses constitutional history evidencing the intention of the Founding Fathers, and of Chapter 4, which considers the decisions of the Supreme Court relevant to the issue.

Are such grants of legislative power avoidable? Is Congress unable to draft and enact statutes that are laws in the true sense, that express rules of conduct? This is the subject of Chapter 5, which describes the legislative process of Congress, the staff assistance available to the national legislature and its committees, and the extent to which this assistance is being effectively used.

Chapter 6 recommends a procedure that, if adopted and followed by the President and Congress, should reduce materially or halt the trend that has been described and help restore an important cornerstone of the constitutional doctrine of separation of powers.

There are two appendixes. Appendix I is a copy of the American Bar Association resolution of 1973. Appendix II describes procedures that several other countries follow: Great Britain, France, Belgium, Austria, and Switzerland. (An illustration of the German procedure is introduced by example in Chapter 5.) For ease of reading all notes follow the text.

Because the sources cited throughout the book are drawn chiefly from legal authorities, they are cited in accordance with the style set out in A UNIFORM SYSTEM OF CITATION (Cambridge, Mass.: Harvard Law Review Association, 13th Ed., 1981), which is authoritative in the legal profession. Further, it is anticipated that readers pursuing further study will be directed to law libraries and better served by legal citation.

However, Chapter 3 (Constitutional History) draws also upon sources normally accessible outside the legal profession. Thus, the citations in that chapter are made in accordance with generally accepted journalistic custom. An exception is made in the case of words capitalized in the Constitution.

Chapter 2

ADMINISTRATIVE AGENCIES AND THEIR DISCRETION*

The chief purpose of this chapter is to indicate the kinds of problems executive departments and independent administrative agencies deal with, how they act with regard to such problems, and whether it is essential to administrative efficiency and the achievement of their statutory objectives that Congress give them policy guidance in those statutes.

While not all legislative delegations of authority to administrative agencies are vague, many are inexcusably so. For comparison, two examples of delegations that supply a specific standard are set forth in the next paragraph.

Section 313(b) of the Communications Act[5] directs the Federal Communications Commission "to refuse a station license" to any person "whose license has been revoked by a court order under Section 313 for engaging in monopolistic practices." Court records are public, and the Commission is left only with the function of factual investigation. A similar example is found in Section 315 involving only slightly broader administrative discretion, but with clear legislative guidance. If a broadcast station permits a legally qualified candidate for public office to appear it must afford equal opportunities "to all other such candidates for that office in the use of such broadcast station . . . ." Here the administrative discretion delegated is that of ascertaining whether the candidate whom the licensee permitted to use the station had "legally

---

*If a statute referred to in the chapter to illustrate the problems raised by excessive delegations of legislative authority was later amended this is not considered relevant for present purposes. The chapter discusses the practical problems by way of illustration only. It is not intended as a critique of particular administrative agencies of the federal government.

qualified" under local or federal law, and whether there had been a permitted "use." Both facts are objectively ascertainable and sufficiently certain and definite. To clarify "use," Congress subsequently excluded appearances by a candidate on a "bona fide newscast," a "bona fide news interview," and other such occasions.[6]

The illustrations that follow, involving several administrative agencies, will deal with Congressional delegations of authority containing much broader discretion.

THE FEDERAL COMMUNICATIONS COMMISSION

The Federal Communications Commission was created by the Communications Act of 1943 to regulate interstate and foreign communications by wire and radio.[7] Radio was interpreted to include television. Later, satellite communication was brought within the Commission's regulatory authority by statutory authorization of the Communications Satellite Corporation for profit and the commercial communications satellite system.[8]

This Commission exercises its authority in the field of broadcasting chiefly through a broad discretion to grant, renew, and deny construction permits and licenses to applicants for radio and television stations, and a broad rulemaking power conferred by statute.[9] It has no jurisdiction over networks, except as they own broadcasting facilities as licensees, or indirectly through FCC regulation of license affiliates. In interstate telephone and telegraph communication, the FCC exercises more extensive delegated authority by virtue of its power not only to grant or deny certificates to common carriers, but also to supervise their rates, territories, and practices.[10]

The FCC regulates entry into broadcasting through a system of licenses, which have various renewable terms: in the case of television, five-year terms; in the case of radio stations, seven-year terms; and in all other cases, ten-year terms.[11] The applicants must state the facts required by Commission regulations as to their citizenship, character, and financial, technical, and other ability; the station's ownership and location; frequencies desired to be used; hours of operation; power; equipment; and other required information.[12] The Commission must make a finding that the public interest, convenience, and necessity will be served before granting an application.[13]

The law further obligates the FCC to make distributions of licenses, and allocations of radio frequencies or wavelengths, of periods of time for operation, and of station power among the several states and communities so as to provide a fair, efficient, and equitable distribution of service, both transmission and reception.[14] The Commission is empowered to issue rules and regulations.[15] It has no power of censorship over communications and may not interfere by regulation with the right of free speech.[16]

Thus the powers of the FCC are broad, lacking in specificity, and its discretion is wide. As the Supreme Court said in an early opinion, "The Act does not restrict the Commission merely to the supervision of the traffic [technical engineering considerations]. It puts upon the Commission the burden of determining the composition of the traffic [programming]."[17]

The statute as shown above sets forth certain legal, technical, and financial matters for the Commission to consider in its regulations for approving license applications. Further, the FCC must find that the public interest, convenience, and necessity will be served[18]—one of the most vague and subjective phrases known to statutory drafters. By way of illustration, when several competing applicants (all meeting the basic statutory requirements) filed for the same television facility, the Commission for many years required the applicants to make comparative showings, under the "public interest" standard, upon what it called the comparative factors, such as the percentage of local ownership represented in each applicant, the percentage of time each applicant's owner or owners would spend at the station (known as "integration of ownership with management"), the proposed programming schedules, diversity of ownership of the media of mass communication (preferring the applicant that represents the fewest radio, television, or newspaper interests), the past broadcast records, the experience of the ownership, the proposed studio facilities, and the amount of local live programming proposed to be scheduled regularly. None of these was otherwise specified by the statute as a licensing factor.

The relative weight that the Commission would give to any particular factor would depend upon a personal judgment based on the record made, rather than a conclusion reached by adding up factor points and comparing scores. Differing views and philosophies of commissioners (or of administrations) on the importance of any particular factor would affect that judgment.

Rarely would a U.S. Court of Appeals disturb a Commission's discretionary decision if supported by substantial evidence (a test easily met), even though the court might disagree with the decision, since the statute placed the discretionary authority in the Commission and not the judiciary. The court ordinarily would reverse only for such reasons as error in the Commission's procedure or Commission action beyond statutory authority.[19] But how difficult it is for a court in a case of this kind to conclude that the administrative agency has acted beyond its statutory power when the statute endows the agency with authority to act in accordance with "the public interest, convenience, and necessity." The court, being unsure what this statutory phrase means, accepts the administrative agency's definition. It should be noted that a recent statutory amendment (Section 309 [i] [1982]) made changes in this longstanding process of comparative hearings by permitting the Commission to make a "random selection" among multiple qualified applicants, provided "significant preference" is given to an applicant that can be expected to promote "diversification of ownership of the media of mass communications" and an applicant controlled by a member or members of a minority group (a legislative policy change, not a change made to avoid legal questions raised by the courts regarding the familiar discretionary points of preference).

Occasionally a decision of the Supreme Court seems to indicate that an agency's authority to make determinations "in the public interest" will not endow the agency with unbounded discretion.[20]

The Democratic National Committee wished to place paid political announcements on the air, and a group opposing the war in Vietnam wished to require a station to accept spot announcements voicing their views. The broadcast stations refused both requests. The FCC upheld the licensees' refusals of the two requests as not raising a "fairness" issue since the licensees had shown equitable treatment of both sides previously as regards each petitioner. The Supreme Court upheld the FCC, holding that its authority to act "in the public interest" must be balanced against the statutory prohibition of censorship and the statutory recognition that broadcast licensees are not government instrumentalities; further, that the FCC power over programming does not include supervision of licensees' editorial expressions or supervision of their day-to-day operations. Chief Justice Burger's majority opinion emphasized that the "public interest" standard must be read to include First Amendment principles prohibiting governmental interference with free speech.[21]

This decision is one of the few placing restraint on the reach of the "public interest" power, the original basis for the "fairness" requirement. Whether its effects will reach beyond the personal freedoms area, which the Court most zealously guards against government invasion, is uncertain.

THE DEPARTMENT OF THE INTERIOR:
MINING OF PUBLIC LANDS

The public land laws of the United States also contain vague statutory provisions. In public land law the government acts as an owner, rather than as a regulator of third parties' actions; hence its exercise of greater authority and discretion is more easily justified. Public land may, as a matter of first impression, seem to encompass a narrow field. This can hardly be so, however, when the volume involved and the diversity of uses are considered.[22]

The laws governing the use and disposition of federal lands have been in the making for 175 years. Many remain on the books, though obsolete. A Public Land Law Review Commission study in 1971 estimated that there are some six thousand relevant laws.[23]

As a response to a "crisis in confidence" regarding its administration, the Public Land Law Review Commission was established by Congress in 1964 to review the public land laws, regulations, and administrative practices.[24] Of the nineteen members of the Commission, six were senators and seven were members of the House of Representatives. After numerous hearings and deliberations the Commission filed a report in 1970 that recommended, among other things, that Congress should state definite policies in the statutes authorizing and directing administration, withdrawal, and disposition of federal lands.[25]

The field of mining law is one the Commission found to be devoid of any legislative policies to guide the administrators. In fact, in this field almost all regulatory rules have been developed only after at least one party has suffered. That is, only in the decision of contested cases at the administrative level under the General Mining Law of 1872 have standards been promulgated as to what the contestants should have been entitled to receive.

Thus current mining law generally provides that "valuable mineral deposits in lands belonging to the United States, both surveyed and unsurveyed, shall be free and open to exploration and purchase ... under regulations prescribed by law. ..."[26] Under the mining law, claims shall not be located until the "discovery" of the vein or lode within their limits.[27]

The statute lacks any policy statement. What are the terms and conditions upon which deposits shall be explored and purchased? This whole subject matter of mining law is left to administrative regulation. The Commission found this one of the most standardless areas it encountered.

By letter to the Director of the Commission on January 20, 1966, Frederic L. Kirgis, a member of the Advisory Council to the Commission, said:

> It may not be an overstatement to assert that the Department (of Interior) through the adjudicatory process, rather than the Congress, has created the mining law as it exists today other than for an original determination that mineral deposits in the public domain were subject to disposition and patent by the Government to the first applicant if he performed some work to prove his good faith and made a discovery (the word "discovery" being undefined and thereby creating one of the most perplexing problems in the administration of the mining law).[28]

Testimony before the Commission[29] emphasized the uncertainties flowing from the absence of legislative prescription:

> In controversial and important subjects such as the definition of "discovery" and the concept of "valuable mineral" the interpretation and application of the law has not been constant and frequently has been inconsistent.

Subsequent testimony of Kirgis as an expert witness before the Commission, focusing in particular on oil shale claims where the greatest known source of energy is involved, most on public lands, shows how grave is the risk of administrative assertion of arbitrary powers.

> There are numerous unpatented oil shale claims many of which are subject to patent application, which have been subject to recent departmental adverse proceedings and some of which are now in the state of litigation. This Commission and the Congress might appropriately consider the status of these claims and, particularly, the administrative imposition of limitations on the concept of discovery as applied to oil shale and the administrative assertion of finality of earlier proceedings involving the claims which were considered by most claimants (but not now by the Department) as expunged by Supreme Court decisions of many years ago.

Considering the gravity of the problem of the oil shale claims and other mining claims, and in view of the fact that the "Constitution gives Congress the basic responsibility for determining the disposition of public lands,"[30] the Commission announced "that Federal statutes should fully prescribe uniform methods by which rights in these resources may be acquired." Its specific recommendation was that

> Congress should establish a fair notice procedure (a) to clear the public lands of long-dormant mining claims, and (b) to provide the holders of existing mining claims an option to perfect their claims under the revised location provisions we recommend.

By such a procedure, the Commission noted that the record would be cleared "of an estimated 5.5 million long-dormant claims." Congressionally enacted criteria to be applied in the administrative processing of the claims, it further found, are also an obvious inherent necessity.

THE ENVIRONMENTAL PROTECTION AGENCY

The Federal Clean Water Act[31] provides inadequate guidance to its administrators or the public. It states a broad congressional goal; to control navigable waters from pollution by prohibiting "pollutants," but neither defines "pollutants" nor provides what range of amounts of waste will pollute. It recognizes that the states have the primary role and responsibility to prevent pollution and develop water resources. However, it requires the states to consult with the Federal Administrator in the exercise of this authority.

The Act requires each governor or state water pollution control agency to review its water quality standards and to modify them "as appropriate," without defining the term. The only statutory guidance provided to the states is that the standards shall consider what will "protect the public health or welfare," "enhance the quality of water," and "serve the purposes of this chapter." The other matters the state shall consider are "their use and value for public water supplies," the "propagation of fish and wildlife," "recreational, agricultural, industrial and other purposes," and finally "the use and value for navigation."

Any new state standard or modification must be cleared with the Federal Administrator, who may compel the state to revise it according to his views of his authority under the Act, which, as noted, is as broad as the subject of water quality itself.

By unspecific language, Congress has delegated statutory authority to an administrator to regulate everyone affected by the subject of water quality. In doing so it has expressly acknowledged, but only by general declarations, that the primary responsibility is in the states.

In contrast, the national legislature has provided expressly that the Administrator may exercise superior authority over the state's actions with respect to water quality. This power, inconsistent with the general declarations previously mentioned, is so vague and all-embracing that the Administrator virtually may, through his "clearance" and "revision" powers, completely subordinate the states to this federal agency in the area of water quality control.

The Administrator cannot know from the language of the statute exactly what decisions he should take on any matter in controversy, whether with a state or with an individual or group. If he forbids the discharge of every suspected chemical into navigable streams he may not be giving due consideration to standards relative to "agricultural, industrial, or other purposes." If he limits his prohibition to chemicals shown by tests *to pollute or likely to pollute* he may, by doing so, offend those advocating a prohibition of any chemical that *may possibly* pollute the water.

THE NATIONAL LABOR RELATIONS BOARD

A statute that has the objective of adjusting equitably the economic balance between two conflicting power groups may ultimately be somewhat more specific than the legislation just discussed. Each group tends to scrutinize amendatory language with care in order to maintain or improve its position. However, because of the conflicting views, compromises in statutory language may be made that leave congressional policy directions to the Executive Branch ambiguous. Judicial review of administrative action may be hampered by uncertainty as to congressional intent. Inconsistent rulings by the administering agency may result, often depending upon the administration in power, and precedent may have little value.

The Wagner Act of 1935 (the original labor relations statute) was enacted because Congress believed that collective bargaining organizations lacked power equal to that held by employers and that this imbalance caused much of the labor strife. By facilitating union representation and promoting collective bargaining, the Act sought to augment employee bargaining power.

During the first twelve years following passage of the law, the balance shifted heavily in favor of unions; this prompted the adoption of the Taft-Hartley Act of 1947 as an amendment. Within the subsequent eleven years Congress found it necessary to enact the Landrum-Griffin Act of 1959 within the same statute, again largely to place restraints upon labor organizations. Together they essentially form the National Labor Relations Act.

Several kinds of unfair labor practices are specified and made unlawful for either employer or employee organizations to commit. For example:

> Employers may not interfere with the rights of employees to organize, may not refuse to bargain collectively with their representatives, and may not engage in discrimination in hiring or tenure to encourage or discourage union membership. Labor organizations are prohibited from refusing to bargain collectively with an employer, from engaging in secondary boycotts, and from coercing employees to join or refrain from joining a labor organization.[32]

Because such provisions are too generally written, too ill-defined, and too ambiguous, the opportunity for arbitrary administrative action or action contrary to the law arises.

A report in 1970 about the National Labor Relations Board, made after public hearings[33] at which testimony was taken by the Subcommittee on Separation of Powers of the Senate Committee on the Judiciary, concluded that the statute had delegated powers to the Board in too broad a manner and that the latter had frequently exceeded its authority. The late Senator Sam J. Ervin, Jr. (D., N.C.), as chairman of the Subcommittee, expressed the further view in 1969 that the NLRB is not alone among administrative agencies needing more definite guidance by statute and supervision by Congress, citing numerous complaints about other agencies, notably the Equal Employment Opportunity Commission and Office of Federal Contract Compliance.[34]

The congressional inquiry turned first to the NLRB because it is an agency that, in the words of the late Senator Everett Dirksen (R., Ill.), "deals with an area of life which is of intimate concern to the individual citizen—that is, the conditions in which he must make his livelihood," and an Agency, noted by legislators to have attracted criticism over the years for its alleged lack of faithfulness to congressional intent.

Testimony was received from three dozen witnesses, including professors of constitutional law, labor relations, and administrative law; attorneys representing labor and management; the Chairman and General Counsel of the NLRB, who testified concerning all matters raised regarding the Board; and a Federal Circuit Court Judge, Henry J. Friendly, who gave his assessment of the roles of the NLRB, the courts, and Congress. The Subcommittee found, in its Report issued February 25, 1970, with one dissent, that the National Labor Relations Act has been accorded inconsistent interpretations and expressions of policy by the NLRB, depending in many instances upon the political party in power, and that these inconsistencies and changes in policy are not due completely to the indefiniteness and breadth of statutory language but are attributable also to failure to read legislative provisions in context or otherwise give effect to intended congressional mandates.[35] Under its authorization, the Board is charged with the duty of applying a complicated act to various factual disputes. Because the statute is a compromise between frequently opposing viewpoints, the Agency has at its disposal sometimes ambiguous provisions of law, reports of committees, and congressional debates related to these provisions that can be read differently by different people; and it has shifted administrative precedents over its long history, to back its decisions. It is often impossible to say that a Board decision is unsupported by any part of the statute.[36]

The dissenting member of the subcommittee considered the NLRB justified since most of its decisions, as the NLRB officials pointed out, had been upheld by the courts when appeals were taken. The difficulty with this view is that the court's review is narrow, as a rule deciding only whether the Board has abused its discretion (not whether it has correctly used it) or whether there is sufficient evidence in the record as a whole to permit a reasoning mind to reach the Board's result (not whether the result is correct or even whether the court thinks the result reached is clearly erroneous). The narrowness of review is provided for in the statute and is a means of preserving the administrative experience and proficiency of the Board from judicial second-guessing, which makes the dissenter's contention (and the NLRB officials') on this point irrelevant. However, if it were made relevant by a statutory provision enlarging judicial review, the vagueness and ambiguity of the statutory policy provisions would stand in the courts' way when they tried to render reasoned decisions on review of Board orders.

One example of recurrent criticism of the NLRB throughout the Subcommittee's hearings is the *Allis-Chalmers* case, involving Section 7 and Section 8 (b) (1) (A) of the National Labor Relations Act.

The Allis-Chalmers Manufacturing Company owned plants in several parts of the country. Employees of two such plants, located in two cities in Wisconsin, were represented by two different unions affiliated with the AFL-CIO. Both conducted economic strikes (which are not unfair-labor-practice strikes, a type protected by the Act) against Allis-Chalmers in support of new contract demands.

Some members of each union crossed picket lines and worked during the strikes. Each union then began internal union actions against those members, charging them with violations of the unions' constitutions and bylaws leading to imposition of fines ranging from $20 to $100 per person. The employer filed a complaint with the NLRB charging unfair labor practices against the two unions.

The unions argued that they were not interfering with the workers' right to work during an economic strike; they were merely imposing internal disciplinary sanctions against their own members as their constitutions provided. The NLRB agreed with the unions by a 2–1 vote.[37]

A panel of the U.S. Court of Appeals for the Seventh Circuit, by divided vote, sustained the Board, but on rehearing upon appeal by the employer, in an *en banc* decision, held that the Board's order could not be sustained.[38] It declared that the statutory provisions, protecting employees' rights to refrain from participation in concerted activities but nevertheless permitting unions to prescribe their own rules regarding "acquisition or retention of [union] membership," were ambiguous when construed together. The court would resort to congressional history to ascertain the intent of Congress. After reviewing reports and hearings of congressional committees that had considered the provisions before enactment, and other legislative history, the divided appellate court decided *en banc* that Congress did not intend by its use of the term "retention of membership" an exercise of the power to fine members, and that had it so intended Congress would have so provided explicitly.

On writ of certiorari, the Supreme Court reversed in a 5–4 decision, holding that the right to abstain from concerted union activities is an absolute right only for nonmembers of a union. Once an employee joins a union, that employee enters into a contract of "full" membership in which he agrees to abide by its rules, and these rules may be enforceable by discipline.[39]

Based on the history of this case, and others it reviewed, and after many days of hearings, the Subcommittee on Separation of Powers issued a report in 1970 concluding that the National Labor Relations Act had delegated powers to the NLRB in too broad a manner, and that the Board had frequently exceeded even this ill-defined authority. Senator Ervin's committee further stated that the NLRB was not alone among administrative agencies needing definite guidance by statute and congressional supervision, being joined notably by the Equal Employment Opportunity Commission and the Office of Federal Contract Compliance.

Another finding of the Subcommittee on Separation of Powers was that the Board had tolerated union authorization cards that are misleading to employees who sign them (under its statutory authority to certify a union as exclusive bargaining agent for employees when the Board determines by an election or "any other suitable method" that the union has majority support). The Subcommittee found that a union may tell employees that signing a card is only an indication that they want to be represented by a union, but not proof that they favor a particular union. The board had explained in a memorandum to the Committee:[40]

> In the absence of coercion, duress or fraud, or misrepresentation by the union solicitor regarding the purpose of the card, the Board relies on the employee's overt action in signing the card as an honest expression of his purpose. The Board believes that respect for the intelligence of employees permits no less than this.
>
> ... In *Cumberland Shoe* the Board held that cards are valid expressions of an employee's selection of a union to represent him, unless the union solicitor represented to the signer that the card would be used only for a Board election.

The *Cumberland* rule adopted by the NLRB, as explained in its memorandum referred to above, was cautiously cleared by the Supreme Court in 1969.[41] Additional administrative policymaking and policy shifting have followed in its wake.[42]

THE DEPARTMENT OF HOUSING AND URBAN DEVELOPMENT

This Department (HUD) was created by statute in 1965.[43] At its core was the Housing and Home Finance Agency (HHFA). Under a reorganization plan of President Truman in 1947, HHFA was given control over several agencies that were responsible for the nonfarm housing assistance of the federal government, including the Federal Housing Administration (FHA), begun in 1934 under President Roosevelt, and the Public Housing Administration (PHA), created in 1937 under the name United States Housing Authority.

The first slum clearance and redevelopment aid was instituted by the Housing Act of 1949,[44] though it had an earlier genesis in the slum clearance and low-cost housing fathered by President Hoover in 1930. In 1950, the Community Facilities and Service of federally aided public works, later called the Community Facilities Administration, and the Federal National Mortgage Association were transferred to the HHFA. During President Eisenhower's administration the 1954 Housing Act added the concepts of rehabilitation and conservation to slum clearance and established urban planning assistance.[45] Succeeding years brought continuation and development of other federal housing and urban activities under the Department.

Arguably adequate standards provided in the earlier acts appear to have given way to statutory opportunity for the exercise of nearly complete HUD administrative discretion.

As illustrations, first, contracts for important urban renewal (federal loan and grant), public housing (federal loan and annual subsidy), and federal housing insurance assistance were made contingent upon local adoption and enforcement of minimum standard housing codes *deemed adequate by and to the satisfaction of the administrator* (emphasis added); and second, urban renewal financial assistance for slum clearance purposes was made contingent upon *the Administrator's determination* that rehabilitation would not equally serve the purpose (emphasis added).[46] That the government's administrator must have power to make decisions in relation to government contracts is not questioned; that there are no standards to govern those decisions in such important local areas of concern, however, raises serious questions of whether the Administrator is making laws as well as executing them, and, in addition, whether there is an undercutting of the constitutional concept of federalism by subordinating local authorities' jurisdiction to the Administrator's discretion.

A further illustration of a grant of large discretion to the Secretary of HUD is this definition in Section 101 (b) of the Housing and Community Development Act of 1977:

(8) The term "extent of poverty" means the number of persons whose incomes are below the poverty level. Poverty levels shall be determined by the Secretary pursuant to *criteria provided by the Office of Management and Budget, taking into account* and *making adjustments, if feasible and appropriate* and *in the sole discretion of the Secretary, for regional or area variations in income and cost of living,* and *shall be based on data referable to the same point or period in time.* [Emphasis added.]

This definition is completely imprecise. It does not furnish an objective standard for the exercise of executive discretion. Two kinds of discretion are delegated: the first is to the Office of Management and Budget to provide criteria of an undefined nature as the basis for poverty levels; the second is to the Secretary, which is equally subjective and is confined to the Secretary's "sole discretion." Yet the above definition is a key to many grants of power to guide the Secretary in distributing funds to metropolitan areas and urban counties throughout the country that apply for federal aid.

In the Federal Demonstration Cities and Metropolitan Development Act of 1966,[47] Congress stated that improvement of urban life is "the most critical domestic problem facing the United States." The Secretary was authorized to provide for locally prepared and scheduled programs to enable cities to "plan, develop and conduct programs to improve their physical environment, increase their supply of adequate housing for low and moderate-income people, and provide educational social services vital to health and welfare."

The Secretary's drafters thus proposed that Congress convey this kind of nebulous authority to HUD in order to give the Secretary any kind of flexibility desired to cope with varying kinds of applications from localities throughout the United States. As the administration proposed, Congress disposed. Upon what was referred to by Congress as the "most critical domestic problem facing the United States," HUD obviously needed greater legislative direction than it received, or requested.

Similarly, provisions of the Demonstration Cities Act administered by HUD do not provide guidance to a locality wishing to qualify. Congress has adopted administration-sponsored language establishing no fixed criteria, leaving it to local agencies to prepare financial requests "containing new and imaginative proposals" to rebuild or revitalize large slum and blighted areas.

Moreover, as has been observed earlier in connection with housing assistance, terms such as "moderate-income people" and "educational and social services vital to health and welfare" have varying meanings depending on the user's background, experience, and social or political philosophy. This obscurity of meaning is not elsewhere clarified in the statutues. They therefore state either no policy, or at best a subjective one. The term "low-income" is defined in the statute by reference to more objective criteria, but this cannot be said for the words "families of moderate income" or "lower income," and hence the terms roam at large.

How is "moderate income" or "lower income" to be determined? The plain answer is that it is whatever the Secretary of HUD says it is. Thus, in testifying before the House Banking and Currency's Subcommittee on Housing on the administrative proposal introducing the term into federal statutes in 1961, the Housing Administrator responded to a probing question of a Sub-committee member, disturbed by the vagueness of the key "moderate-income" term, as to whether a member of Congress could be eligible as a person of moderate income.[48] The response was in the affirmative. That the question needed to be put is as startling as the response. The language became part of the law enacted as the Housing Act of 1961.

In the early 1950s the meaning of the statutory term "fair value for use in accordance with the redevelopment plan" in the Housing Act of 1949 came into intra-agency question.

The administrative interpretation was important because of the amounts of federal loan and grant money involved. This depended in part upon the deficit that urban renewal projects sustained between, on the one hand, the purchase price paid by a local public agency for the purchase of slum properties plus the cost to it in demolishing the improvements and installing utilities and streets, and, on the other, the return the local public agency received from private developers when it resold this land for reuse in accordance with the use restrictions provided in the city's redevelopment plan.

The statute provided that resale would be made at the "fair value" of the land for such use.[49] If "fair value" were interpreted to mean "fair market value," this construction in each transaction would be based upon principles established and recognized by the courts of law over an indefinite number of years and in countless kinds of circumstances. This interpretation, if adopted, would act as a guide to federal administrators in approving the amount of federal subsidy eligible for payment to the locality (matched by a lesser local contribution), since an integral element in determining the local deficit would be the "fair value" the locality must obtain for the site.

If a different construction were adopted and fair value for the new use specified in the redevelopment plan were administratively found to be a sui generis provision of the statute, "fair value" would become a very subjective term. It might, for example, take into consideration social and economic benefit to the community in enticing new industry to the city—a value impracticable of computation. Or it might be considered some subjective figure per lot that "moderate-income families" could be expected to pay (if the planned reuse were restricted to this undefined group of people). The legislative history of the statute offered no clue as to how "fair value" should be determined.

The judicial "fair market value" concept, on the other hand, takes into account the kinds of uses that may be made of the property, and hence it could be applied in determining the "fair value for use in accordance with the use provided in the redevelopment plan."

The Housing and Home Finance Agency's legal staff recommended that the "fair market value" concept be adopted as the meaning intended by Congress when it used the term "fair value." The administrative staff opposed this recommendation as unduly restricting administrative flexibility and impeding the implementation of urban renewal policy.

The real problem? Congress had enacted a statute establishing a new social "program" with unclear, ambiguous provisions inadequately setting forth legislative policy. The resulting risks? The Treasury may be exposed to heavier calls if the fair value is too depressed, leaving excessive disparity between the resale fair value and the cost of original acquisition; conversely, if the fair value is established at too high a figure, the social purpose of the federal program may not be carried out. Since fair value of land frequently has been judicially construed as meaning its "fair market value" taking into consideration the use for which it is intended and adopted, the advantage of accepting this interpretation would be to achieve the congressional purpose while retaining access to judicial precedents as a guide for future administrative interpretations in the variety of situations to be expected to arise.

DELEGATION OF THE POWER TO DECLARE WAR

The joint congressional resolution referred to as the Tonkin Gulf

Resolution[50] was adopted by Congress by a vote of 502 to 2 on August 7, 1964, just three days after the alleged engagement on the night of August 4, 1964, between two U.S. ships, the *Maddox* and the *Turner Joy,* and several North Vietnamese vessels.

The resolution stated in part[51]

> That the Congress approves and supports the determination of the President, as Commander in Chief, to take all necessary measures to repel any armed attack against the forces of the United States and to prevent further aggression. . . .

> The United States regards as vital to its national interest and to world peace the maintenance of international peace and security in Southeast Asia.

> The United States is, therefore, prepared, as the President determines, to take all necessary steps, including the use of armed force, to assist any member or protocol state of the Southeast Asia Collective Defense Treaty requesting assistance in defense of its freedom.

The parties to the Southeast Asia collective defense treaty (SEATO, or Southeast Asia Treaty Organization) of September 8, 1954, were Australia, United Kingdom of Great Britain, France, New Zealand, Pakistan, the Philippines, Thailand, and the United States. A protocol on Indochina[52] additionally provided that the economic and defense measures and protections of the treaty should also apply to the States of Cambodia and Laos and the free territory under the jurisdiction of the State of Vietnam.

Secretary of Defense McNamara, in discussing the operative sections of the resolution, believed ". . . it to be the generally accepted constitutional view that the President had the constitutional authority to take at least limited armed action in defense of American national interests."[53]

Undersecretary Katzenbach in the Senate hearings referred to the passage of the resolution as amounting to "the functional equivalent . . . to declaring war."[54]

Years later Senator James Fulbright and other members of Congress who approved the Tonkin Gulf resolution criticized U.S. embroilment in Vietnam. However, much of the criticism was self-directed. As Senator Fulbright told the Separation of Powers Subcommittee of the Senate Judiciary Committee:[55]

The fundamental mistake, however, was in the giving away of that which was not ours to give. The war power is vested by the Constitution in the Congress, and if it is to be transferred to the Executive, the transfer can be legitimately effected only by constitutional amendment, not by inadvertency of Congress.

A letter of Congressman Abraham Lincoln to his law partner William Herdon in 1848 states in part:[56]

Allow the President to invade a ... nation whenever he shall deem it necessary to repel an invasion, and you'd know him to make war at pleasure. ... You may say, to him, "I see no probability of the British invading us;" but he will say to you "Be silent; I see it, if you don't."

The events were a foreseeable, potential consequence of congressional failure to scrutinize and limit the breadth of power delegated to the President in the joint resolution, protocol and treaty; and together with subsequent appropriations and other ratifying actions of Congress they made up the declaration of war required by the Constitution, as courts later held.[57] The resolution, standing alone, may not be characterized as the equivalent, functionally or otherwise, of a declaration of war under the Constitution.

SUMMARY

The preceding discussion deals with only a few examples of partial legislative abdication of power or overly broad delegation of authority to the executive. The effects indicated—in public assistance for housing of the poor and the elderly, in labor relations, in the public broadcasting media, in the production of and conservation of public lands, in avoiding pollution, in the exercise of the war power—assume substantial proportions when multiplied again and again in other legislative areas.

Did the Founding Fathers intend by the Constitution they adopted to require that when Congress thus delegates powers it shall couple the delegation with standards whereby the Executive can intelligently perceive how they are to be administered? This question is the subject of the next chapter.

Chapter 3

CONSTITUTIONAL HISTORY

A Congressional statute instructs an administrative agency: "Here is the problem; deal with it." Does such a statute, transferring the solution of national problems to the executive, comply with the letter of a constitution that directs that "all Legislative Powers herein granted shall be vested in . . . Congress. . . ."? If the statute is deemed to comply with its literal command, does this language conform with the spirit of the constitutional document?[58]

That Congress is virtually exercising this choice of using broad terms that implicitly delegate "Legislative Powers" to agencies was illustrated in Chapter 2.

Chapter 3 will review relevant parts of the history of the Constitution, indicating the intentions of the Founding Fathers, in order to determine whether this choice is consistent with the intent of that document.

INTRODUCTION

As noted in Chapter 1, Section 1 of Article II of the Constitution vested all legislative powers granted by the Constitution in Congress. In determining whether Congress should provide actual standards or policies when it delegates responsibilities to federal administrative agencies, we must go first to the time nearly 200 years ago when the constitutional provisions were drafted, debated, and adopted. Our effort is to learn what the Founding Fathers who produced, and the citizens who ratified, the document intended by such a declaration. Did they mean to prohibit the legislative branch from delegating its lawmaking power to the executive or judicial branch? If so, what did they mean by legislative power? And what prevents Congress from redelegating the legislative powers vested in it?

Another important avenue of historical inquiry is the intent of the adopting fathers and the ratifying people in the novel designation of three great branches of government and concurrent separation of them, that is, by stating in three segregated articles, in what is known as the separation of powers doctrine, that the legislative power should be given to one branch, the executive power to another, and the judicial power to the third. Would it be consistent with that statement if Congress (hypothetically) were to enact a series of laws transferring one-half of all of its legislative powers to federal administrative agencies created by those statutes; for example, passing on to them general power to regulate the national economy as they see fit? Were the constitutional provisions for checks and balances, which complement the separation of powers doctrine by giving each branch some governmental participation outside its own sphere (for example, the presidential veto power), designed to justify legislative conferment of broad and ill-defined powers upon the executive branch and federal administrative agencies generally? We may find bases for answers to such questions in the debates of the Founding Fathers at the Constitutional Convention of 1787, which adopted the Constitution of the United States, or in THE FEDERALIST PAPERS, which later explained the Constitution for the benefit of the states that had yet to ratify or reject that instrument of national government.

Examination of constitutional history is indispensable for anyone intent upon establishing the true meaning of the provisions of the document. It would be optimistic to expect to discover specific answers to current questions. Ours is a broader inquiry: to find the intent and policies that led to the adoption of provisions such as are referred to above. To the extent that we can find illumination of this sort for the constitutional language, we are better able to correct substantial deviations, if any, from its commands.

The terms of reference of the Constitution will be first discussed, since they are pertinent to the scheme of organization of the federal government, which in turn is of inescapable concern to the subject of discussion. Attention was given, in perfecting that scheme, to (1) meeting the need for fighting the War of Independence, (2) remedying the defects of the Articles of Confederation, (3) preserving the sovereign powers of the states to the extent compatible with achieving (1) and (2), and (4) generally, assuring the liberties of individual citizens, particularly in light of their earlier experience with tyranny and despotic rule.[59]

The Articles of Confederation

The first term of reference was also the first written general constitution, the Articles of Confederation, and it had been the only attempt[60] to satisfy the primary objectives mentioned above, and to carry on that war. As established under the Articles of Confederation, Congress was given exclusive power to make war and peace, to negotiate treaties and alliances, to send and receive ambassadors, to try cases of piracy and felony committed on the high seas, to fix standards of weights and measures, to regulate Indian affairs, and to establish and operate a nationwide postal system. On matters of great importance, specified in the Articles, the vote of two-thirds of the states was required to authorize Congress to act. Among the specific areas mentioned were declaration of war, confirmation of treaties, regulation of the value of coinage, borrowing and appropriation of money, and development of land and naval forces.

Though the Confederation Congress was ineffectual in persuading the states that greater powers were needed by the central government, certain problems required immediate and decisive attention. Virginia and Maryland took independent action on mutual problems of commerce on the Potomac River at a meeting at Mount Vernon in 1785. At the close of the meeting, Maryland proposed that an interstate council meet at Annapolis in September of the next year to discuss problems of commerce affecting all of the states. Only five states, Virginia, Pennsylvania, Delaware, New Jersey, and New York, did, in fact, attend. Thus the Annapolis Convention had proved to be an extralegal committee reminiscent of the Continental Congresses of the 1770s, and the Confederation Congress refused to extend to it official recognition. In November 1786, the Virginia legislature adopted an official resolution appointing delegates to a convention that the Annapolis delegates had suggested be scheduled to meet in Philadelphia in May 1787; and the national lawmakers urged all of the states to do likewise. In a short time, with the approval of the Confederation Congress, all of the states except Rhode Island had nominated delegates to what was later to be known as the Constitutional Convention of 1787.

To these men, what was needed was a new *form* of Union based on an entirely new concept. That concept was one of national authority derived from the *people*, as opposed to one derived from the state legislature. Thus authority, we shall see, was to be directly responsible to the people, and so constructed internally as to render it impossible for any branch of that national authority to usurp the authority of the other branches and thereby become supreme and potentially tyrannical. Moreover, although the principle was not expressly to be stated in the document that defined the national government, it was understood that the sovereignty of the national government would not encroach upon the autonomy of any of the several states, the two spheres of operation being distinct. The lack of an explicit statement guaranteeing certain powers to the states caused considerable alarm throughout the states, which was quieted (and ratification of the Constitution by the states obtained) only by the appending in November 1791 of the first ten amendments to the Constitution. The Tenth Amendment reads:

> The powers not delegated to the United States by the Constitution, nor prohibited by it to the States, are reserved to the States respectively, or to the people.

THE CONSTITUTIONAL CONVENTION OF 1787

Prepared and agreed upon by fifty-five delegates from twelve states at a constitutional convention held in Philadelphia from May 14 to September 17, 1787, the Constitution of the United States was ratified by the required nine states by July 1788. It would become the framework under which a people were both to govern and to be governed. The Founding Fathers attempted to construct a workable system of rules that would balance the interest of the people individually with the concerns of the states (or the people in a collective capacity).

The Constitution[61] that emerged from the Philadelphia Convention, as we know, was much more than an amendment of the Articles of Confederation to supply important omissions. The War of Independence (concluded by the Treaty of Paris in 1783 giving international recognition to the independent new nation) had clearly demonstrated that the government of the republic must be sufficiently strong to maintain its political integrity and that the other defects of the Articles must be remedied. The sovereign powers of the states must be preserved to the extent compatible with achieving this national necessity. Finally, it was understood that the new nation had broken from England because despotic and tyrannical encroachments upon its citizens had become intolerable; therefore there should be safeguards against excessive interference by government with personal liberties and property, and with state administration.[62]

Among the chief concerns of the delegates at Philadelphia were to what extent the sovereignty of the states would survive under the new Constitution and whether the interests of the smaller states would be protected against the political strength of the larger states in the election of the national legislature.

The second issue was compromised acceptably by providing for equal representation of the states in the Senate and proportional representation of the states in the House of Representatives. The first issue presented more difficulties.[63]

The first issue was resolved satisfactorily by providing for a national government of limited powers. As mentioned above, those powers not delegated to the national government by the Constitution, and not prohibited to the states by the document, were reserved to the states, according to the Tenth Amendment (which, as a part of the Bill of Rights, was proposed to the legislatures of the several states by the First Congress on September 25, 1789, and ratified by the states between 1789 and 1791).[64]

James Madison, Jr., of Virginia felt that these measures, together with the check provided by the people themselves, should dispel any fear of aggrandizement of federal power, but he was equally convinced that it was improbable that they would.[65] Therefore auxiliary precautions must be taken.

Allocation of Powers

A division of power was provided within the central government. A second precaution, already noted, was an acknowledgment of the reservoirs of power vested in the states and in the people themselves. Both proposals were accepted. The framers believed that if they could divide the national authority into three autonomous branches, as had been done in state constitutions, and if each of these branches possessed a particular function with built-in defenses and powers to prevent dominance by another branch, then these provisions, coupled with the power reserved to the states, would effectively prevent the new central government from achieving ascendancy over its citizens.[66] The following constitutional provisions applicable to the branches furnish examples of how the founders acted upon this belief, and there are others that will go unmentioned here.

Article I, Section 1, of the Constitution provides:

All legislative powers herein granted shall be vested in a Congress of the United States, which shall consist of a Senate and House of Representatives.

Article I, Section 8, Clause 18, provides that Congress shall have power

to make all laws which shall be necessary and proper for carrying into execution . . . .

other powers granted, such as the power to collect taxes, borrow money, coin money, declare war, establish a uniform rule of naturalization, create uniform laws on the subject of bankruptcies, and regulate commerce with foreign nations and among the states.

Article II, Section 1, of the Constitution provides:

The executive Power shall be vested in a President of the United States of America. . . .

Section 2 provides that "The President shall be Commander in Chief . . ." and confers upon the President the pardoning power, the power to make treaties by and with the advice and consent of the Senate, the duty to nominate and, by and with the advice and consent of the Senate, appoint judges of the Supreme Court, the power to veto legislation (subject to veto override by two-thirds vote of each house), and other powers and duties.

Section 3 provides:

The President may call special sessions of Congress on extraordinary occasions, and that he shall from time to time give to the Congress information on the State of the Union, and recommend to their consideration such measures as he shall judge necessary and expedient. . . . he shall take Care that the Laws be faithfully executed. . . .

Article III, Section 1, provides:

The judicial power of the United States, shall be vested in one Supreme Court, and in such inferior Courts as the Congress may from time to time ordain and establish. . . .

Article III, Section 2, provides:

The judicial Power shall extend to all Cases, in Law and Equity, arising under this Constitution, the Laws of the United States, and Treaties made. . . .

Separation of Powers

The doctrine of separation of powers is, and was to the Convention delegates, important in two respects. First, internally the constitutional provisions that are its source divide the responsibility within the federal government into three distinct branches. Second, the division was intended to preserve state sovereignty.

The concept of dividing federal powers among three branches of government—legislative, executive, and judicial—was not a novel one insofar as the delegates were concerned. A similar separation of powers doctrine had been advocated some years before by the highly acclaimed French political philosopher, Baron de Montesquieu, in his work THE SPIRIT OF THE LAWS, which was published in 1748.[67] Foster Hall Sherwood in 1941 referred to the THE SPIRIT OF THE LAWS as the "analysis of government which served as authority in the debates on the adoption of the Constitution."[68] James Madison credited Montesquieu with being the originator of the American version of this doctrine.[69] The Supreme Court has affirmed the intent of the framers that this doctrine is an established part of our Constitution.[70]

The French jurist and philosopher stated the need for a separation of the powers of government so that all, or two, might never be fused in one. He said that unless there was a check on governmental power tyranny would result. Having only recently survived a crisis precipitated by the tyrannical actions of a British monarch, the delegates felt a unique appeal in keeping governmental powers in balance and in check, coupled with the due process protections that the Bill of Rights would contemporaneously provide through the Fifth and Fourth Amendments of the Constitution.

The relevancy of Montesquieu's writings to the issues discussed in this book is evident. If Congress can delegate its legislative power to the executive by statute after statute, the doctrine of separation of powers breaks down, and the risk of tyranny in government becomes real, for one branch divests itself of basic power by transferring the power, without constitutional authority to do so, to another branch.

As Montesquieu said, and the Founding Fathers believed and intended to provide against:[71]

> When the legislative and executive powers are united in the same person ... there can be no liberty; because apprehensions may arise, lest the same monarch ... should enact tyrannical laws, to execute them in a tyrannical manner. ...

> Again, there is no liberty, if the judiciary power be not separated from the legislative and executive. Were it joined with the legislative, the life and liberty of the subject would be exposed to arbitrary control; for the judge would be then the legislator. Were it joined to the executive power, the judge might behave with violence and oppression.

Accordingly, the legislative, executive, and judicial branches are provided for in separate and distinct articles in the Constitution, thus by necessary implication carrying out the concept of separation of powers.[72]

Checks and Balances Provisions

Each department was also given a constitutional means of checking the other, so that, in Madison's words,[73] "Opposite and rival interests ... may be sentinel over the public rights. ..."

As we shall see, Madison went further, explaining that the security against encroachment would be enhanced by further provisions, which have also been referred to as internal checks and balances:

> It is necessary to introduce such a balance of powers and interests as will guarantee the provisions on paper. Instead, therefore, of contenting ourselves with laying down the theory in the Constitution, that each department ought to be separate and distinct, it was proposed to add a defensive theory in practice. In so doing, we did not blend the departments together. We erected mutual barriers for keeping them separate. ...[74]

Thus at a point in the debates, after the structure of the Congress had been discussed, it was decided that the House of Representatives would share in the supreme judicial power. Impeachment of the national executive and other government officials was to originate in the House. The Senate was to be the judge and jury in impeachment trials over which the Chief Justice would preside. The Congress could from time to time establish inferior courts to share in the judicial power of the United States.

The Senate would have what, under British tradition at least, was considered to be a power of the executive, in that a two-thirds vote of the members present was required to ratify a treaty. The national executive was named Commander-in-Chief of the armed forces, and the Congress had control of their activation and the number of men to compose them; and the appropriations to maintain them could be projected only for two years.

The national executive was given the power to execute the laws, but he was restrained by the knowledge that he could be impeached by the House and tried by the Senate. The most important interaction power of the executive protects his office from encroachment: the executive has a qualified negative on acts of the Congress, known as veto power.

The judicial power of the United States is vested in one Supreme Court and in such inferior courts as Congress may establish. This power extends to all cases arising under the Constitution and laws of the United States or under treaties made, and to other enumerated cases and controversies. The judges who make up the national judiciary obtain their places through initial nomination by the executive and confirmation by a vote of the Senate of two-thirds of the members present. The salary of the judges is fixed by law according to a specific constitutional provision to this effect, and the salary cannot be reduced during their term of office. The guiding principle for this provision, say THE FEDERALIST PAPERS, is that a ''power over a man's substance amounts to a power over his will.''[75]

Thus the Founding Fathers also showed their intention that the branches of government should not operate in watertight compartments, each separate in all ways from the others.[76]

Powers of Congress

No evidence is found, however, demonstrating that the desirable harmony among the three branches, or the possibility of overlapping power situations (a subject again discussed in Chapter 4), or other reasons would justify interbranch interference with a basic function specifically assigned by the Constitution, such as the power of Congress over federal legislation. In fact, any inference that may be drawn from constitutional history, as will later appear, denies any authority in Congress to delegate a basic legislative power to another branch, and thus to share its legislative jurisdiction.

Article I, Section 1, of the Constitution provides:

> All legislative powers herein granted shall be vested in a Congress of the United States, which shall consist of a Senate and House of Representatives.

Legislative powers are not confined to the eighth section of Article I, in which a list of enumerated subjects[77] is set down under the heading: "The Congress shall have power." Discussion of both the legislative and executive branches will deal mainly with their chief powers, and with these (beyond mentioning them) only as they contribute to the issue under discussion.

With regard to the powers conferred upon Congress by Article I, most of the debate in the Convention centered, as might be expected, on the effect of these provisions upon the sovereignty of the states. Insofar as the war power was concerned, though a few favored placing this power in the executive, the majority considered it too important a power, having too great a consequence upon the nation, to bestow upon one person.

The spending and taxing powers are specifically and exclusively conferred upon Congress by Article I, Section 7, of the Constitution. Not only is the money power one of the lawmakers' strongest, but, being specifically conferred, it may not be redelegated to another branch.

Penal Laws

During the debate on the wording of the clause of Article I, Section 8, that confers power on Congress to define and punish piracies committed on the seas and offences against the Law of Nations, attention was focused at one point upon whether the language was sufficiently specific for a subject such as criminal conduct, and particularly such conduct among nations. No idea of a redelegation by Congress was introduced into the discussion. Questions were raised concerning use in the Constitution of words having vague or ambiguous meanings in a delegation of power to Congress to declare the action of an individual a felony. George Mason referred to the "strict rule of construction in criminal cases"; however, the view of Madison and James Wilson prevailed, that[78] "strictness was not necessary in *giving authority* to enact penal laws *though necessary in enacting or expanding them*" (emphasis added).

Since strict rules of construction obviously, in the nature of things, could not be applied in the instance of vague delegations of statutory authority, the necessary inference is that Congress, not the Executive, may expound what constitutes criminal conduct. Congress accordingly may make no broad statutory delegations of power to the Executive insofar as the definition and punishment of crimes are concerned.

Necessary and Proper Clause

Article I, Section 8, provides that Congress shall have power

To make all laws which shall be necessary and proper for carrying into execution the foregoing powers, and all other powers vested by this Constitution in the government of the United States, or in any department or office thereof.

The words "necessary and proper" sometimes are cited to support a contention that they enable Congress to delegate its legislative powers at will, and particularly in order to meet more efficaciously the demands of a modern, complex world.

The explanation of the "necessary and proper" clause in THE FEDERALIST PAPERS, from a general referencing to the text, shows that the clause was intimately connected with the phrase "supreme law of the land."

Both clauses caused considerable disturbance in the ratifying conventions and among private interested citizens. The principal objection to them lay in the apparent broad grant of power. However, as Alexander Hamilton says,[79]

It would be absurd to doubt that a right to pass all laws *necessary* and *proper* to execute its declared powers would include that of requiring the assistance of the citizens to the officers who may be entrusted with the execution of those laws as it would be to believe that a right to enact laws necessary and proper for the imposition and collection of taxes would involve that of varying the rules of descent and of the alienation of landed property or of abolishing the trial by jury in cases relating to it.

According to Hamilton, then, the essential point to be developed is that "the propriety of a law, in a constitutional light, must always be determined by the nature of the powers upon which it is founded."[80]

Madison's position was similar. His view of the "necessary and proper" clause was that "without the *substance* of this power, the whole Constitution would be a dead letter." Calling to mind the weaknesses of the old government under the Articles, Madison explains:

> As the powers delegated under the new system are more extensive [than the powers delegated to the Congress under the Articles], the government which is to administer it would find itself still more distressed with the alternative of betraying the public interests by doing nothing, or of violating the Constitution by exercising powers indispensably necessary and proper, but, at the same time, not *expressly* granted.

> Had the Constitution been silent on this head, there can be no doubt that all the particular powers requisite as means of executing the general powers would have resulted to the government by unavoidable implication. No axiom is more clearly established in law, or in reason, than that wherever the end is required, the means are authorized; wherever a general power to do a thing is given, every particular power necessary for doing it is included.[81]

> If the different parts of the same [Constitution] ought to be so expounded as to give meaning to every part of it, shall one part of the same sentence be excluded altogether from a share in the meaning; and shall the more doubtful and indefinite terms be retained in their full extent and the clear and precise expressions be denied any signification whatsoever? For what purpose could the enumeration of particular powers be inserted, if these and all others were meant to be included in the preceding general power? Nothing is more natural nor common than first to use a general phrase, and then to explain and qualify it by a recital of particulars.[82]

This general provision had also been a part of the former Articles of Confederation, and Madison pointed out that it could have no more meaning in the Constitution than it held in the Articles, which were accepted universally as granting inadequate power to Congress.

Thus there was no intention on the part of the founders to bestow a new, basic, and independent power on Congress by the "necessary and proper" clause—no thought of granting an authority having no relationship to the other powers provided in the Constitution. Its applicability, in Hamilton's words, would turn upon the nature of the power sought to be brought within the clause; in Madison's exposition, the clause would apply to bring within its terms powers *indispensably* necessary to perform the express powers. The clause permitted legislative action of a similar nature, reasonably incident to that authorized by the express powers, but did not permit legislative abdication of constitutionally provided duty and responsibility to legislate. The inescapable conclusion is that the clause conferred no power upon Congress to delegate its own power to promulgate legislative policy—a power legislative in nature—to the Executive. Moreover, such a delegation would be contrary to the separation of powers doctrine of the Constitution since under the Constitution the President has the responsibility to execute the laws. To combine the function of executing the laws with that of enacting them would be an unconstitutional mingling of functions not countenanced by the separation of powers doctrine.

Powers of the Executive

The national executive was an innovation of the Philadelphia Convention, inasmuch as the Confederation Congress had to execute its own laws. In the Philadelphia Constitution the executive was a single individual, the President of the United States, who was to "execute" the laws of the United States.

His powers were rather narrowly defined and in general were limited to the administration of federal laws: as provided in Article I, Sections 1 and 3, the executive power shall be vested in a President, who must take oath (or affirm) that he will faithfully execute the office and preserve the Constitution of the United States to the best of his ability, and take care that the laws are faithfully executed.

There are exceptions to the above generality, which by express provision permit the President to participate in the legislative function. This participation occurs in two principal instances, treaty making[83] and the qualified veto power. In the first instance, the executive is empowered to make treaties, but only "by and with the Advice and Consent of the Senate . . . provided two-thirds of the Senators present concur." The second form of this participation in the legislative function occurs in the case of the qualified veto of any and all legislation enacted by the legislature. The President is permitted to veto any legislation his sympathies do not support. This provision in turn is also significantly qualified by a provision that enables Congress to reconsider all such vetoed legislation, and pass it over the veto with a two-thirds concurrence of each of the two houses.

These two instances are a portion of the checks and balances that the Constitution provides. The essential function of the executive branch was and is to carry out the law.[84]

This presents the question: What should be the nature of executive power in carrying out this essential responsibility? Mr. Madison attempted to obtain resolution of this problem.

The Fate of the Madison Motion

On June 1, 1787[85] the Committee of the whole House agreed to consider the seventh resolution submitted by Mr. Randolph concerning the executive. It provided in part, "Resolved that a national executive be instituted . . ." The quoted first clause of Randolph's resolution was agreed to. Members of the Committee then discussed whether the executive should be one person, a question on which there was division of opinion. A suggestion having been made, this issue was deferred. Madison stated his view that the members first fix the authority the Executive should have before making a choice between "a unity and a plurality in the Executive."

Accordingly, Madison moved, with a second by Wilson, that "the national executive shall have *power to carry into effect the national laws*, to appoint to offices in cases not otherwise provided for, *and to execute such other powers as may from time to time be delegated by the national legislature*"[86] (emphasis added).

General Charles Pinckney, of South Carolina, suggested a limiting amendment of Madison's proposal by inserting in the final clause after the words "such other powers" the words "not legislative nor judiciary [sic] in their nature." Madison accepted the suggestion and all members of the Committee concurred. The last clause of Madison's motion, as thus amended, read, "and to execute such other powers not legislative or judiciary in their nature as may from time to time be delegated by the national legislature." Pinckney, who had suggested the limiting amendment, then objected to the final clause of the Madison motion, as thus limited. The clause, permitting Congress to delegate additional power—not legislative or judicial in nature—to the President, was voted down by the Committee.[87]

Pinckney's objection was solely to the last clause of the Madison motion, including his amendment underlined in the preceding paragraph, beginning with the words "and to execute such other power..." The Committee, by majority vote, agreed with him that once Congress was prevented from delegating powers legislative or judicial in nature, the executive would as a consequence be confined to exercising executive power. Since the first clause of the motion—without the delegation clause—authorized the executive to carry out the national laws, no more was needed.

The majority of those speaking on the general questions of a single versus a plural executive and the powers the executive should be given were of the view that the Executive's main power should be to execute the laws as they came from the legislature. Pinckney, John Rutledge of South Carolina, Roger Sherman of Connecticut, and James Wilson of Pennsylvania all expressed their belief in the vigorous leadership by a President in carrying out laws that Congress enacted. Wilson, for example, desired "energy dispatch and responsibility," but declared that the prerogatives of the British monarch were not a proper guide in defining the executive powers inasmuch as, "[S]ome of these prerogatives were of a legislative nature..."

These statements do not suggest that the delegates were inclined to permit delegations of power of a "legislative or judicial nature" to be made by Congress to the executive.

The important points are: First, the reasonable inference may be drawn that Madison, Pinckney and other founders believed it would be improper for Congress to delegate to the executive any powers which were either legislative or judicial in their nature. The Committee intended Congress alone to be the policy maker, to express the will of the people through laws. The debates showed this. And they showed that the Committee intended the executive to execute and to carry out that will, but not to form it. The forepart of Madison's motion, that "the national executive shall have power to carry into effect the national laws," satisfactorily stated their intention. To go further, they feared, might give the executive authority, for example, over war and peace. Second, having established this proposition, Pinckney successfully objected to the last clause of Madison's motion as limited by Pinckney's own suggested words. Pinckney was unwilling to add an unnecessary (because the power of the national executive had been sufficiently set forth in the preceding clause of Madison's motion) and ambiguous provision to the Constitution.

It is sometimes contended, in defense of extensive congressional delegations to administrative agencies illustrated in Chapter 2 and elsewhere, that Pinckney and Madison had deemed it "unnecessary" to provide Congress with specific authority to add to the President's executive powers under the Constitution. However, constitutional history read in context clearly demonstrates that this is not correct. When the Founding Fathers used the word "unnecessary" with reference to the Madison motion they were using the word in the context summarized in the preceding paragraphs and the note accompanying this paragraph.[88]

The delegates objected to imprecise constitutional wording. Thus, the day before, May 31, when a proposal was made to give Congress "legislative powers in all cases to which [sic] the State Legislatures were individually imcompetent," Pinckney and Rutledge disagreed with the wording. They "objected to the *vagueness* of the term 'incompetent,' and said they could not decide how to vote until they should see an exact enumeration of the powers comprehended by this definition."[89]

Madison said he "did not know that the words were absolutely necessary [to retain]... " but he did not "see any inconveniency in retaining them, and cases might happen in which they might serve to prevent doubts and misconstructions".[90] However, Pinckney's motion to strike the delegation portion of Madison's resolution prevailed by a vote of 7 to 3.

From the foregoing it is reasonable to conclude that if a power is legislative in its nature it must be exercised by Congress and may not be delegated by Congress to the executive. The Founding Fathers foresaw that such a delegation provision, even when amended to exclude powers legislative or judicial in nature, would create a Pandora's Box. What does "legislative or judicial in their nature" mean? Would powers specifically vested in Congress by the Constitution be deemed "legislative in their nature" -- such as the legislative power to approve treaties and executive and judicial appointments -- or would they fall within the delegateble powers? How would the basic concept of separation of powers be affected? Might it be rendered meaningless? These are but a few of the obvious, predictable questions which might be invited through adoption of such an ambiguous provision for delegation of power to the executive if frozen into the Constitution.

This is far from saying that the founders had not considered where powers should be assigned among the branches. A consensus existed to allocate the basic powers among branches, keeping those branches for the most part separate and specifying in which branch certain powers belonged, as elsewhere appears. But there is a clear distinction between a grant *to Congress by the people* of the authority to legislate without defining the lawmaking power (leaving it to the legislature to give meaning to that authority), and a grant to Congress by the people of the authority to bestow that power elsewhere. That distinction struck at the heart of the Madison motion; its passage could introduce a method of circumventing the doctrine of separation of powers.

The Constitution remains in the form thus advocated by General Pinckney. Section 1 of Article II provides: "The executive power shall be vested in a President of the United States of American . . ." Section 3 of Article II in pertinent part provides: ". . . he shall take Care that the Laws be faithfully executed . . ."

The executive carries out the law under this constitutional authority. Federal statutes enacted by Congress pursuant to its constitutional authority provide, as a matter of course, the authority necessary for their administration.

Having begun with the most general grant of power to the executive, we will now consider illustrations of the particular powers conferred on that office.

Particular Powers

(1)

Article II, Section 1, of the Constitution states in part:

The Executive Power shall be vested in a President of the United States of America . . .

and further requires that the President shall take an oath or affirmation that he

will faithfully execute the Office of President of the United States, and will to the best of [his] . . . Ability, preserve, protect and defend the Constitution of the United States.

Section 3 in part provides that

he shall take Care that the Laws be faithfully executed. . . .

The power of the Executive to execute faithfully the laws of the Union was essential to the concept of the executive. It was contained in the Virginia Plan of Randolph, who, however, conceived of the executive as three men, sitting in council. The provision next appeared in the JOURNAL in the August 6 Report of the Committee of Detail, in William Paterson's Plan (the New Jersey Plan), and again in the draft of the finished Constitution presented to the convention on September 12. The provision was expressed in various ways:

1. *Virginia Plan:* "that besides a general authority to execute the National laws. . . ."

2. *Report of the Committee of the Whole:* ". . . with power to carry into execution the National Laws;"

3. *New Jersey Plan:* ". . . besides their general authority to execute the Federal acts. . . ."

4. *Constitution as reported August 6:* "he shall take care that the laws of the United States be duly and faithfully executed."

5. *Constitution as reported September 12 and 17:* "he shall take care that the laws be faithfully executed."

There was no significant debate on this point, the convention agreeing with Madison's observation of June 1 that "certain powers were in their nature Executive, and must be given to that department whether administered by one or more persons. . . ."[91]

The description of the executive branch of the central government by Hamilton in THE FEDERALIST PAPERS does not cover in detail powers of that branch. Hamilton is concerned primarily with assuring the citizenry that the executive branch, as constituted by the "supreme law of the land," meaning the Constitution, is "energetic" enough to promote a good administration and consequently a good government, but "safe" enough not to breed a tyrant.[92] Hamilton lists, and does not comment on, the power of the president to commission officers of the United States[93] and the power of the president to "take care that the laws be faithfully executed."[94] However, with regard to the latter power, Hamilton does implicitly explain it in the following argument:[95]

Energy in the Executive is a leading character in the definition of good government. It is essential to the protection of the community against foreign attacks; it is not less essential to the steady administration of the laws; to the protection of property against those irregular and high-handed combinations which sometimes interrupt the ordinary course of justice; to the security of liberty against the enterprises and assaults of ambition, of faction, and of anarchy.

(2)

There is one instance in Article II, dealing with the delegation of mixed powers, in which there are expressed the conditions for the legislature as one of the participants to delegate a discretion to the President, to the "courts of law," or to the "heads of departments." This is the power of appointment in Section 2, whereby the President shall

nominate, and, by and with the advice and consent of the Senate, shall appoint ambassadors, other public ministers and consuls, Judges of the Supreme Court, and all other officers of the United States, whose appointments are not herein otherwise provided for, and which shall be established by law. But the Congress may, by law, vest the appointment of such inferior officers as they think proper in the President alone, in the courts of law, or in the heads of departments.

The delegates to the Convention agreed that the power of appointment was an executive function. On June 1, Wilson said that "the only powers he conceived strictly Executive were those of executing the laws, and appointing officers not appertaining to and appointed by the Legislature."[96]

The breadth of the power of appointment became an issue again before the Convention on August 24. Sherman voiced his opposition in the draft of the clause

and shall appoint officers in all cases not otherwise provided for by this Constitution.[97]

He said that he thought it was proper that the executive appoint men to offices in the executive branch and otherwise if they were not to be appointed by a special constitutional provision. However, he "contended that many ought not be, as general officers in the army in this time of peace, etc."[98] He therefore moved that "or by law" be inserted after the word "Constitution." Madison made a slight change in the wording "officers" to "offices" "in order to obviate doubt that he might appoint officers without a previous creation of the offices by the Legislature."[99] But Sherman's motion did not pass. A more restrictive wording was proposed by John Dickinson, which did carry:

> and to all offices which may hereafter *be created by law*[100] (emphasis added).

There was discussion as to the power of appointment being "a formidable one both in the Executive and Legislative hands ..." so that when the clause was reported out of the Committee of Eleven on September 4, the power of appointment was to be shared by the Executive and the Senate. Sherman said vehemently that "Good laws are of no effect without a good Executive; and there can be no good Executive without a responsible appointment of officers to execute."[101]

Gouverneur Morris of Pennsylvania, a member of the drafting committee, answered that "as the President was to nominate, there could be responsibility, and as the Senate was to concur, there could be security."[102] The wording was accepted after the insertion of "and counsel" had been made.

Article II, Section 2, of the Constitution states in part that the

> President shall be commander-in-chief of the army and navy of the United States, and of the militia of the several states, when called into the actual service of the United States.

The basic issues in the debate as to this more specific power did not center around the propriety of the executive's command of the army and navy, for it was considered that command of the nation's forces must be an executive function. The issues more closely resembled those of today.

On August 17, the members of the convention decided that it was the executive's duty to "make" or "conduct" war; therefore, with the paramount intention of preventing cabal, they made it a legislative power to "declare" war.[103]

Hamilton pointed out[104] that the power of the Commander-in-Chief, as granted to the Executive by the Constitution, is quite limited, first by the fact that he is in command only when the militia is called out according to "legislative provision." And, compared with the power of the British monarch, who can declare war, the President is significantly limited in that he will have "the supreme command and direction of the military and naval forces" only at the discretion of the legislature. Further,[105]

> the direction of war implies the direction of the common strength; and the power of directing and employing the common strength forms a usual and essential part in the definition of the executive authority. . . .

However, he concluded that "it is the nature of war to increase the Executive at the expense of the Legislative authority."

Hamilton's observation is supported by enactments of Congress from that day until this, delegating the broadest kinds of power to the President in wartime, war emergencies, or defense treaties. Examples include the War Powers Acts during World War II and the Gulf of Tonkin Resolution during President Lyndon B. Johnson's administration.

THE STATE RATIFYING CONVENTIONS

With only the crudest of communications available, the new Constitution became public knowledge in a surprisingly short time. Newspapers in Philadelphia and Lancaster had printed the complete text by September 19, two days after the Convention ended. German translations were available in Pennsylvania Dutch regions the same week, and by the end of October virtually every adult American had read it, even backwoodsmen.

Many delegates believed that centralization of authority in a national government would imperil individual freedom. Others contended that the states would no longer have responsibility over their local affairs, and a new king would be substituted for the English monarch.[106] Some were worried that certain states would obtain economic and political advantages over others. Delegates weighed a number of other arguments, some technical in nature, against individual provisions of the Constitution. Patrick Henry was a fierce opponent in Virginia, where his oratory bowed to Madison's logic. John Randolph, though he had refused to sign the document, supported its ratification. In New York, Hamilton and John Jay were leading protagonists. THE FEDERALIST PAPERS, written by Madison, Hamilton, and Jay, were available to all and were effective in persuading minds open to argument, as many were. The universal respect for George Washington also was a pro-Constitution force.

Advocates of the Constitution at these conventions rebutted the arguments of their opponents with reasoning that differed only in detail from the views discussed heretofore. The favorable votes received in some states were close. The explanations given presumably carried weight, demonstrating insofar as is pertinent to our subject the care with which the document had been drafted in order to avoid the tyrannies of the past. Proponents argued that adequate powers were vested in the proposed national government, but no more than it needed to discharge its task. They assured the people that control was reserved to the states over their internal affairs, and they explained that the government being established would consist of three branches, together with specification of the powers of each branch and a division or separation drawn among them to prevent the combination in one of the powers belonging to another or all three.

In the state ratifying convention of Connecticut a general concern for the effect the power to tax would have upon the states was allayed in the debate. An equally strong argument was persuasively made for the separation of powers among the branches of the federal government.

The debates in other states followed the same outline. In Delaware, Massachusetts, Maryland, South Carolina, and New Hampshire, as in Virginia and New York, there was a great anxiety that local power of the states or the people would be lost with the creation of a new federalist form of government as distinguished from the old confederation.

This was substantially eased by the necessity for a general government and the strong provisions for separation of powers adopted from the writings of de Montesquieu. In addition, by the time of the concluding debates, it was understood that the first task of Congress should be the consideration of a Bill of Rights as an amendment of the Constitution. Presumably, had New York and Virginia not raised and fought bitterly over this concept, they would not have ratified the Constitution.[107]

SUMMARY

With this history, may Congress delegate to the executive branch, including the President or any administrative agency known today, power to lay and collect taxes, duties, imposts, and excises? This is an express and specific power reposed by the Constitution in Congress, and the answer should be "no."

May Congress delegate to an administrative agency the power to propose amendments to the Constitution for ratification by the state legislatures or conventions? The answer should be "no," for the same reason. The power to regulate interstate commerce or international commerce? Again the same answer. The power to declare war? No, in the express words of Hamilton, as we have seen; and since the words are from THE FEDERALIST, they were words of reassurance to persuade the ratifying conventions. The power to enact a law? Again no, since this is the most basic legislative power: witness the founders' rejection of a Madison motion providing for legislative delegation of powers but excluding powers of a "legislative or judiciary nature."

There is ample justification in the history for the interpretation that the founders intended that powers either legislative or judicial in nature shall not be delegated to the executive. An amendment, construed as possibly having this effect, was rejected by the founders for this reason. It is particularly relevant when read in conjunction with the allocation of different powers to the branches and the careful, thoughtful reasons that moved the framers in the course of this assignment. The assignment assuredly was a part of their effort to preserve the concept of separation of powers, which they so vigorously espoused not merely as a constitutional objective but as a fundamental requirement. This reinforces the validity of the conclusion drawn. If a power is legislative in nature it must be exercised by Congress and it may not be delegated by that branch to another branch. The power to make laws, and to establish legislative policies, is such a power. What a law is, what constitutes a legislative policy, is less clear. The founders, and THE FEDERALIST PAPERS, in their explanations as to why certain grants of governmental authority were made to the first branch and others to the second branch, and regarding the degree of dependence they considered essential that each have upon the other, supply some additional guides. The Supreme Court has given other guidelines to help us answer this question, which will appear in the next chapter. How far they take us in resolving what has become a controversial issue, as has been noted in grants of legislative power discussed in the preceding chapter, is evidenced by leading decisions of the Supreme Court, which are discussed in Chapter 4.

Chapter 4

SUPREME COURT DECISIONS

INTRODUCTION

The Supremacy Clause of Article VI makes the Constitution, and all federal laws and treaties that are made pursuant to that document, the supreme law of the land, binding all state courts, and overriding any contrary provisions in their constitutions and statutes. But this applies only to federal laws appropriate to the central government under the Constitution's provisions. The attention of the Philadelphia Convention in providing for a Supreme Court had been upon the necessity for judicial review in order to enforce the Supremacy Clause in this context. So, there was room for argument on the question, which later developed, of whether the Supreme Court should be the arbiter of the Constitution when no controversy was present respecting federal versus state supremacy. Could the Supreme Court of the United States declare unconstitutional any statute enacted by Congress and signed by the President, or was the Court merely a coequal branch bound by a statute that had, in form at least, followed the processes required by the Constitution?

This question was settled by the Supreme Court in an opinion written by Chief Justice Marshall in 1803. Since Section 1 of Article III provides that "[t]he judicial power of the United States shall be vested in one Supreme Court, and in such inferior courts as the Congress may from time to time ordain and establish," the Court in *Marbury v. Madison* held that it had power to review congressional statutes and declare them unconstitutional. Marshall's view may be paraphrased thus: If a written document must be interpreted, the judiciary is the proper organ so to do and to declare the constitutionality or unconstitutionality of the act or conduct involved.[108]

Supreme Court justices have told us in very general terms how they approach the task of interpreting the Constitution. Chief Justice Marshall stated: "The subject is the execution of those great powers on which the welfare of a nation essentially depends. . . . This provision is made in a Constitution intended to endure for ages to come and, consequently, to be adapted to the various crises of human affairs." Similarly, Chief Justice Stone in this century wrote: "We read [the Constitution's] words, not as we read legislative codes which are subject to continuous revision with the changing course of events, but as the revelation of the great purposes which were intended to be achieved by the Constitution as a continuing instrument of government."[109]

One of the early decisions of the Court involved an issue of separation of powers. According to *Little v. Barreme*,[110] powers that the Constitution assigns to one of the three branches of government may be exercised only by that branch. A power that falls somewhere between powers assigned to two different branches (an overlapping power) may be exercised by either of the two branches. However, as the paramount branch because of its unique position of closeness to the people as a whole, Congress, alone among the three branches of government, can assign powers where doubt exists concerning which branch under the constitutional separation of powers provisions should have jurisdiction over the power. This matter came to the attention of the Supreme Court in the early nineteenth century. The Court concluded, in holding invalid an action of the President that conflicted with a subsequent act of Congress, that when the three branches of government have overlapping powers (that is, two or more branches each have some reason to make a constitutional claim to the power), the *legislature* can permit exercise of the same power by each branch or can assign it to one (including itself) to the exclusion of the other.

The constitutional doctrine of separation of powers, already discussed, has been recognized as controlling by the Supreme Court. The checks and balances provisions receive like recognition. There is no reasoned analysis of the kinds of powers that must be kept separate, particularly when the contention is that Congress has delegated its own legislative power to the executive.

Such a delegation actually raises a two-pronged question. First, has Congress delegated a power granted by the people to Congress alone, a power that the lawmakers had no authority to redelegate to another branch, including the Executive? Second, is the concept of separation of powers violated when the effect of a statute is to unite legislative powers of the first branch with executive powers of the second branch? The decisions that follow show how the Supreme Court has disposed of the above two-part issue.

JUDICIAL CATEGORIES

Discretion to Find Facts

One of the earlier decisions of the Supreme Court on this subject, *Field v. Clark*,[111] which came down in 1892, held that if Congress establishes the statutory policies to be followed it may delegate to the Executive the responsibility of making determinations of fact involving exercise of discretion. The exercise of certain administrative discretion is necessary in executing a law, and this power may be delegated constitutionally. Every directional detail need not be expressed in a federal statute delegating authority to an administrator.

A federal statute fixed the tariff on imports and exempted certain countries from the tariff charges. It also provided that if the President found that exempt countries were charging duties on exports by U.S. merchants he should proclaim a suspension of the exemption, thereby reinstating the rates established in the statute against these countries.

The statute was upheld since it expressed the legislative policy that tariffs should be charged, set forth in what amounts and with what exemptions, and described the circumstances under which exemptions should be suspended. Whether this policy would apply depended on whether contingencies specified in the statute occurred, a fact that the President could be granted discretion to determine. The further discretion involved in executive interpretation of the edicts of foreign countries required only the objectivity of the expert, and found precedent in many statutes Congress had enacted without question for the past hundred years.

Provision of an Intelligible Principle

A delegation of broad powers to the Executive will be sustained if the power is delegated in terms providing an intelligible principle and direction for the official to follow.

Field v. Clark was carried a step further by *J.M. Hampton, Jr., & Co. v. United States*,[112] a leading decision announcing the principles that

Congress should follow in delegating authority to the Executive. This case, which involves more than determining that a contingency has become fact, deals with both foreign and domestic tariffs. It serves as a good modern starting point on all questions of delegation of legislative power.

A 1922 statute delegated power to the President to raise or lower the tariff provided in the statute in order to enable domestic producers to compete equally with foreign producers of similar articles in U.S. markets. Maximum and minimum figures were provided in the statute, beyond which the President was not authorized to change the statutory rate. He could act only after investigating and comparing the costs of local and foreign production, and after considering differences in wages, costs of material and other production costs at home and abroad, differences in wholesale prices, advantages to foreign producers from their governments, and any other advantages or disadvantages in competition.

The flexible tariff provisions were attacked in an action brought by an affected party when the President increased the tax on imported barium dioxide from $0.04 to $0.06 per pound. The Supreme Court upheld the statute, concluding that since the law laid down an "intelligible principle" that the executive must apply in changing the tariff rate there was no unconstitutional delegation of legislative power.

A statutory rate ceiling for increase or decrease was provided. Changes in the tariff were required to be based upon statistical data, and though the work of obtaining and comparing costs of local and foreign production would be considerable and the results perhaps only roughly accurate, it was feasible to perform it in an equitable manner, presumably through research of field officers abroad. The hearing procedures required by the statute would provide assurance that the administrative determination was reasonable. Thus, the statute provided an objective standard to guide and limit the administrative official in his exercise of statutory discretion.

Imputation of a Meaningful Standard

Another early line of judicial decisions upheld, as a legislative standard, such terms as "fair and reasonable," "unfair and unreasonable," and "discriminatory," as applied to federal regulation of rates and charges by public utilities, such as telephone and telegraph. However, this terminology, on its face giving insufficient guidance to regulators, has had a long history of special meaning in the courts, which gave it content as part of the law governing public utilities that is applicable to suits regarding charges of railroads for the carriage of goods, and similar utility controversies. These terms had acquired judicial meanings that the Court assumed were known to and intended by Congress when it enacted the later laws.[113] And at the time that was not an unreasonable presumption. Terms such as "unfair competition" or "unfair methods of competition," which the Federal Trade Commission was granted power by the legislature to restrain, received similar treatment from the courts as analogous to the use of similar condemned practices at common law as demonstrated in the tort, fraud, and antitrust cases.[114] Thus, the Court said in effect that the statute was enacted in light of and in conformance with the judicial principles of the past and that these principles may be read into the statute to supply the otherwise missing legislative standards.

The Court accorded similar treatment to statutes that conferred broad authority upon the executive to take charge of the affairs of federally chartered savings and loan associations that were financially insecure, unstable, and mismanaged. A statute [115] gave the Federal Home Loan Bank Board

> full power to provide in the rules and regulations herein authorized for the reorganization, consolidation, merger or liquidation of such association, including the power to appoint a conservator or receiver to take charge of the affairs of any such association, and to require an equitable readjustment of the capital structure of the same; and to release any such association from such control and permit its further operation.

The Supreme Court in a 1947 opinion by Mr. Justice Jackson, reversed an injunction granted against the Bank Board, which had taken over an association.[116] Again, the theory was that insolvency had derived a special meaning known to the legislature from numerous judicial precedents and intended by Congress as a guide to and limitation of the administration.

When the courts uphold statutes that authorize administrative agencies to grant certificates of public interest, convenience, and necessity to railroads and other carriers, the same principle is involved, as Professor Jaffe has reminded us. They do so upon the premise that history and custom give meaning to these terms as they relate to public utilities, and that the meaning reaches back to the common law of England, was imported to the colonies, and is a part of our legal tradition, thus well known to Congress when it used the terminology.[117]

This judicial reasoning should not be applied in fields of administration bearing no similarity to the areas in which the judicial definitions originated. Unfortunately, some statutory phrases that have been considered as possessing an acquired meaning, such as the term "fair and reasonable," have more recently been upheld as objective terms in dissimilar areas of activity, without regard to their historical lineage. Such terms, when no longer employed in a judicially defined sense or in accordance with their historically understood meaning, become as elastic and indefinite as the subjective tastes of the regulator. Thus what may be fair and reasonable to the mind of the consumer may not be fair and reasonable so far as the supplier is concerned.

Once the congressional delegation of power is extended to a field far removed from those with which the courts are familiar, the judiciary fails in its own responsibility if it clothes subjective or indefinite "standards" with objective precision. The standards in the statute that circumscribe administrative discretion must be reviewed on their own merits. Unless other provisions of the statute (or legislative history or judicial usage) clothe them with the necessary contours of legislative policy, as exemplified under the next topic, they should not be enforced.

"The Public Interest" as a Standard

A common example of the kind of delegation about to be considered is a statute authorizing the Federal Radio Commission (now the Federal Communications Commission) to issue licenses for conducting an interstate buiness operation subject to the government's determination that the public interest, convenience or necessity will be served by granting the application for license. As we have seen earlier, if the term is used in the context with which the courts or legislature are familiar and thereby has attained a special meaning, there is little problem. The administrators can interpret their statute according to that meaning, or by analogy to that definition. Should the "public interest," however, be used by Congress as a standard for administrative determinations in a statute regulating a novel and developing field of activity, the administrators cannot turn for help to custom or legal tradition. People have different conceptions of the public interest.

The Communications Act, as we have seen, contains such language and involves government regulation of a novel area of business. The term did not stand alone, however. Applicants, according to the statute, must also be found to be legally, technically, and financially qualified to be granted licenses. The law further obligated the administrative agency to make allocations of radio frequencies or wavelengths, of periods of time for operation, and of station power within zones for radio broadcasting service, both of transmission and reception throughout the country. The Commission was directed to equalize broadcasting licenses, bands of frequency, and wavelengths within these zones and among the states by maintaining allocations of licenses according to population upon a "fair and equitable" basis.

The administrative tribunal investigated the number of licensed radio stations in all of the states and in the several interstate zones and adopted general orders determining what would constitute "fair and equitable" allocations of stations among the states, and which states and zones on this basis were over or under their quotas, insofar as location of broadcasting stations and like statutory criteria were concerned. It took into consideration the capacity and power of existing stations in arriving as its determination of what would be a fair and equitable allocation of licenses, wavelengths, and so on to each of the states. Other provisions in the statute dealt with the elements that should enter into Commission findings of this kind, such as the requirement that it take into consideration the changing of periods of time for operation and for increasing or decreasing station power, and similar matters.

Federal Radio Comm. v. Nelson Bros. Bond and Mortgage Co.[118] involved a controversy in which an Indiana station applied for a license that would cause direct interference with the operations of an already FRC-licensed Illinois station, which strongly objected. After a hearing, the agency ruled in favor of the Indiana applicant since the state of Indiana, under the Commission's previously adopted general orders, had been found to be under quota and the state of Illinois over quota in the distribution of local radio licenses. The Supreme Court of the United States, in 1933, held that the Commission had acted within its power and that the statute under which it acted was constitutional. The Court concluded that the delegation by the Congress of the power to grant or deny license applications on the ground of finding of public interest, convenience, or necessity was constitutional "in the context" of this statute. Mr. Chief Justice Hughes's opinion described the Agency's task of allocating frequencies on the basis of geographical and equitable distribution as firmly required by the policies written into the statute. The facts in issue related directly to this specific policy. The controversy involving an applicant in an under-quota state and a station in an over-quota state brought into direct focus the statutory policy of equal distribution of licenses among the states. The determination made by the Commission, that it would be "in the public interest" to grant the application from Indiana, applied the allocation policy expressed in the law. When other provisions of a statute clothe the term "public interest, convenience, and necessity" with meaning, the Court holds, public interest "in context" (in the context of those provisions) constitutes an adequate standard. This is far from holding that the term standing alone would have been upheld. Other provisions expressed the legislative policy required to sustain the delegation. An "intelligible principle" was found and followed by the Agency.

However, some of the later decisions, and some commentators, tend to disregard the qualifying language "in context" that was important to the Supreme Court's validation of the statute involved in the *Nelson Bros.* case, and this is a significant omission.[119] It accounts for the conclusion expressed in some of the recent court holdings and in many writers' treatment of the subject of delegation of legislative power (and perforce constitutional provisions for separation of powers) as a dead issue. Thus, they say, it is constitutionally valid for a statute to authorize an administrative agency to make determinations based solely on "the public interest."

If the public interest alone is an adequate standard for delegating legislative power to the executive, Congress equally might delegate to administrators such powers, without other definitive directions, as responsibility for improvement of agricultural income or for stabilizing the economy or for revitalizing urban communities. And then it will become very clear that Article I of the Constitution, placing the power to make laws for the federal government in Congress alone, has been emasculated.

War Power and Conduct of Foreign Affairs

A World War II case, *Lichter v. United States*,[120] presented a delegation-of-powers question due to a statutory provision that the United States should recover "excess profits" from war contracts that it had entered into with private contractors. The Renegotiation Act, enacted in 1942, provided for a renegotiation of government contracts entered into in the future, or not yet performed, by the War Department, the Navy Department, or the Maritime Commission. The power to renegotiate was to be exercised whether or not the government had retained such a right in the contract. The secretaries of the departments affected were directed by the Act to renegotiate contracts whenever, in their opinion, "excessive profits" had been realized or were likely to be realized from any such government contract on which final payment had not been made. It was provided that the Bureau of Internal Revenue should assist each secretary for the purpose of making examinations and determinations with respect to profits. If it was found that a part of the contract price represented "excessive profits" already paid, the government was authorized to recover them. There was no express definition of the term "excessive profits." Affected contractors claimed that the government's findings of "excessive profits" were invalid. Might not, for example, a federal administrator with previous experience in private enterprise take a different view of whether profit is excessive than an administrator without experience in the problems of meeting a payroll?

The Supreme Court in its decision relied in great measure upon the war power. It quoted from the Preamble, from Article 1, and from Article 2 of the U.S. Constitution, relating to the need to provide for the common defense and the maintenance and support of armies and navies, and the power of the President as the Commander-in-Chief. The Court gave considerable emphasis also to the provision of Article 1 empowering the Congress to make all necessary laws to carry out such powers. The Court felt that, of all the powers in the Constitution, the power that related to the defense of the nation was the strongest and firmest base from which Congress could construct necessary and proper laws. Alexander Hamilton's forceful words in THE FEDERALIST PAPERS were referred to:[121]

> The circumstances that endanger the safety of nations are infinite, and for this reason no constitutional shackles can wisely be imposed on the power to which the care of it is committed. This power ought to be co-extensive with all the possible combinations of such circumstances and ought to be under the direction of the same councils which are appointed to preside over the common defense.

Another factor involved in this case, less emphasized in the lengthy opinion, is the judicial recognition that:

> In 1942 the imposition of excess profits taxes was a procedure already familiar to Congress, both as an emergency procedure

to raise funds for extraordinary wartime expenditures, and to meet the needs of peace. The recapture of excess income as applied by Congress to the railroads had been upheld by this Court in 1924. . . .[122]

Clearly the tribunal was drawing meaning from judicial and legislative history.

J.W. Hampton, Jr., & Co. v. United States,[123] discussed earlier in another context, gave special consideration to the needs of the President for broad authority in another dual and overlapping power situation, that of foreign affairs, and to the large number of statutes, dating back to the founding of the Republic, that bestowed extensive power on the President in matters involving foreign affairs and that the Supreme Court was loathe to disturb. In foreign affairs, the President is again exercising not one, but two powers bequeathed him by the Constitution; not only does he execute the law, he also is engaged in the conduct of foreign affairs, a second express grant of power. Moreover, it is a kind of power uniquely suited to exercise by single leadership.

How far the Court will go to uphold delegations affecting foreign relations is shown by the case of the *United States v. Curtiss-Wright Export Corp.*[124] (1936), when it decided that such a grant of power by joint congressional resolution to President Franklin D. Roosevelt should be overturned only if found to be unconstitutional beyond all rational doubt.

The resolution in that case gave the President the authority to prohibit by proclamation the sale of arms in the United States to certain South American countries if he found that prohibiting the arms sale to the countries ''now engaged in armed conflicts in the Chaco ...'' may ''contribute to the reestablishment of peace between those countries.'' A criminal penalty was provided for violation of the President's proclamation.

The President issued a proclamation setting forth the required findings on the very day of congressional approval of the resolution of authority, which proclamation prohibited arms sales to Bolivia and Uruguay. The validity of a conspiracy indictment against the defendant in the *Curtiss-Wright* case was sustained by the Supreme Court over an objection of unlawful delegation of legislative power. The Court expressly restricted its holding to circumstances of foreign affairs. It pointed out that only the President could negotiate with foreign countries, and secret discussions and holding information in confidence appeared necessary. Hence, Congress could well believe that it was proper to lay down only general standards by which presidential action should be governed.[125] The Court's opinion found a kind of inherent presidential power in this area, emphasizing that unlike domestic powers, the states never had possessed international powers; hence these must have been transferred to the federal government from another source—namely, the Crown, then the Union, and after adoption of the Constitution the federal government itself—as a necessary part of sovereignty, whether enumerated in the Constitution or not.

Certainly an exceptional reason was needed for the validation of a delegation so subjective as the determination of whether an action "may contribute to the reestablishment of peace among a number of countries."

On more recent occasions, also, the Supreme Court has affirmed that a more liberal judicial construction is warranted in cases involving foreign affairs. In June 1984 the Supreme Court upheld in *Regan v. Wald*[126] a Treasury Department embargo regulation issued in April 1982 under the broad power delegated to the chief executive to impose comprehensive embargoes on foreign countries by the Trading with the Enemy Act of 1963 as carried forward by a grandfather clause in the International Emergency Economic Powers Act of 1982. The regulation substantially limited travel of U.S. citizens to Cuba. One of the issues was whether the freedom-to-travel protections of the Due Process Clause of the Fifth Amendment were violated by the regulation. The decision stated:

> In the opinion of the State Department, Cuba, with the political, economic, and military backing of the Soviet Union, has provided a widespread support for armed violence and terrorism in the Western Hemisphere. . . . Given the traditional deference to executive judgment "in this vast external realm" . . . we think there is an adequate basis under the Due Process Clause of the Fifth Amendment to sustain the President's decision to curtail the flow of hard currency to Cuba currency that could then be used in support of Cuban adventurism—by restricting travel. . . .[127]

The Court cited *Zemel v. Rusk*,[128] a 1965 decision, in holding that the Fifth Amendment right to travel, standing alone, is insufficient to overcome the foreign policy justifications supporting the administratively imposed travel restrictions.

The Power to Impose Criminal Sanctions

A comment in the Columbia University Law Review in 1943 observed that "the power to declare a crime is not a mere detail but is a policy question constituting the essence of the legislative power."[129]

As we have seen in the constitutional history portion of this text, the Founding Fathers intended that only Congress should have the power to declare violations of federal statutes or regulations criminally punishable, and their intention has been respected. No administrative agency has been delegated that authority; Congress can provide (and has provided) that a violation of the statute or of the regulations that it has authorized the executive branch to adopt shall constitute a crime punishable by a defined maximum fine or maximum term of imprisonment. But the statute must *contain* this provision; it may *not* delegate the authority to the agency to provide (or not to provide) that violations of its orders or regulations shall be thus punishable.

Only sketchy statutory standards to guide the Secretary of Agriculture were provided by a forestry statute that came before the Court in *United States v. Grimaud*[130] (1911), one of the first cases to present the question of whether an individual could be criminally prosecuted for violation of regulations made by a public official. The government prevailed. *Grimaud* involved an indictment of a sheep man for grazing sheep in a forest reserve without a permit required by the regulations of the Secretary of Agriculture. The statute provided that the Secretary of Agriculture could make the rules and regulations to ensure the improvement and protection of the national forests, regulate their occupancy, secure favorable conditions of water flows, and furnish a continuous supply of timber for the necessities of the citizens of the United States. It further provided that any violation of the statute or of rules and regulations of the Secretary shall be punished by a maximum fine of $500 or a term in prison of not to exceed twelve months, or both, at the discretion of the Court.

The supreme Court first decided that the government should have, and be able to delegate, greater discretion in the operation of property it owns than it should have with respect to the regulation of the property of individuals,[131] and drew an analogy to the liberal exercise of the police power by states and local communities. It then held that the power to declare conduct criminal, which is one of the most important legislative powers, had not been delegated to the Secretary since the statute provided that a violation of the Secretary's regulations would constitute a crime.

The punishment also was provided in the statute. This statutory provision applied not only to violations of the law; it also applied expressly to violations of such regulations as the Secretary under his delegated authority should issue in carrying out the law. Therefore in the latter respect Congress had stated its will.

The questions would have been quite different if Congress had given the Secretary discretion to make some violations crimes and others not; here a policy would not be stated by Congress but would be left with the official. Nevertheless it is evident, since the statute had reference to rules to be adopted in the future, that the Secretary had broad discretion to establish the rules whose violation could lead to conviction. Since criminal enforcement would be by way of prosecution, any illegal application of this discretion could be cured by the trial court, and the facts relative to violation would be the province of the jury. The rules that were violated were required to come within the statutory standards and to be a reasonable application of them. The court defers to the legislative judgment in order to permit enforcement of statutes in the manner Congress has determined to be necessary or desirable. All of these facts presuppose that the legislative judgment is embodied in the provision of an intelligible principle which as has been seen is frequently not the case.

What kind of violation will be thus punishable need not be provided in the statute. Some statutes speak of "willful" violations of statute or regulations; others of "willful or gross" violations; yet others add the alternative adjective "repeated"; or there may be no adjective, though this is less frequent. Equally important, what kind of regulation will thus be punishable need not be provided in the statute. The fact that the statute does not specify the regulation, order, or action that is thus punishable accentuates the grave danger of overbroad delegations by Congress. The breadth of authority it delegates to administrative agencies in many instances permits them to adopt regulations and orders restricting the general public in unexpected ways—violations of which may be prosecuted as crimes. The broader the statutory policies, the broader the areas of individual liberty or property or of economic freedom covered by the statutory policies, the more dangerous becomes the risk of administrative tyranny through adoption of rules and regulations and the delegated power to prosecute those who violate them, as well as the power to select arbitrarily whom to prosecute and whom not to prosecute.[132] Desirable though the delegated power may be for effective regulation, it is more than counterbalanced by the importance of expressing adequately the congressional policies in the statute.[133]

If the statute imparts no real notice of the conduct that may be impermissible, the court trying the asserted violation has no true statutory criteria against which to test the reasonableness of the rule. The practical effect is to delegate the authority to establish crimes. Nearly all of these statutes provide criminal sanctions for violation of administrative rules and orders.

The significance in including this subtopic of crimes is to emphasize that if Congress does not perform its most important responsibility, that of lawmaking, by enacting legislation that is understandable to the public, but delegates the substance of that responsibility to unelected administrative agencies, it is placing individuals in jeopardy of imprisonment or heavy monetary fines or loss of livelihood. The individuals affected may be persons who have no actual notice that they are violating the law, who do not realize that unknown regulations of unknown agencies have become the law that governs them. These regulations are not accessible in a library or law office in many communities.

The Standards of Legal Obligation

A.L.A. Schechter Poultry Corp. v. United States[134] involved a criminal prosecution of the Schechter Company and its officers because they refused to comply with a Live Poultry Code promulgated under the provisions of the National Industrial Recovery Act.[135] The N.I.R.A. authorized the President to approve "codes of fair competition" drafted by an industry if he found it "will tend to effectuate the policy of this title." The President was authorized to impose such conditions "to effectuate the policy" declared "for the protection of consumers, competitors, employees, and others, and in furtherance of the public interest, and may provide such exceptions to and exemptions from the provisions of such code as the President in his discretion deems necessary to effectuate the policy herein declared."[136]

The policy "herein declared" referred to the first section of Title I of the N.I.R.A., which was declared to be "the policy of Congress." It read as follows:[137]

> to remove obstructions to the free flow of interstate and foreign commerce which tend to diminish the amount thereof; and to provide for the general welfare by promoting the organization of industry for the purpose of cooperative action

among trade groups to induce and maintain united action of labor and management under adequate governmental sanctions and supervision, to eliminate unfair competitive practices, to promote the fullest possible utilization of the present productive capacity of industries, to avoid undue restriction of production (except as may be temporarily required), to increase the consumption of industrial and agricultural products by increasing purchasing power, to reduce and relieve unemployment, to improve standards of labor, and otherwise to rehabilitate industry and to conserve natural resources.

The Supreme Court in 1935 unanimously held that the code-making power conferred was an unconstitutional delegation of legislative power. It is impermissible, said the justices, to delegate to the President, in view of the scope of the broad declaration of policy and of the nature of the few restrictions that the Act imposed, "unfettered discretion to make whatever laws he thinks may be needed or advisable for the rehabilitation and expansion of trade or industry." Applicants for approval of a code could "roam at will and the President may approve or disapprove their proposals as he may see fit."

The Court also emphasized that the limitless field of policy left to the President

a host of different trades and industries . . . extending the President's discretion to all the varieties of laws which he may deem to be beneficial in dealing with the vast array of commercial and industrial activities throughout the country. . . .

The government's argument that the statute under attack was an attempt to meet a grave economic crisis that still existed was denied on the ground that economic conditions could not excuse a violation of the Constitution.[138]

The judicial reverse constituted only a temporary setback. The New Deal lawyers formed a bright pool of talent. Once the *Schechter* rule was imposed, the vast area of regulation contemplated by the National Industrial Recovery Act was broken down into legislative segments. Proposal after proposal was sent to Congress by the President, each specifying its own area of operation and containing delegations of administrative discretion that were often questionably "canalized" (to borrow Justice Cardozo's scathing characterization of the N.I.R.A. in *Schechter*). These proposals were to pass muster with reviewing courts in good part due to the narrower subject areas of the statutes, though they included broad delegations of authority. These were enacted one by one, dozens of such statutes, together filling much of the area of domestic regulation originally within the coverage of the National Industrial Recovery Act, now invalidated. The National Labor Relations Act, the Federal Trade Commission Act, the National Mediation Act, the Housing Act for low-income families, the Federal Housing Insurance Laws, the Agricultural Marketing Agreement Act, and the Public Utility Holding Act are examples of laws containing such delegations of power to administrative and regulatory agencies enacted in the wake of *Schechter* occupying parts of the area that the N.I.R.A. was designed in a shotgun pattern to include. These laws survived constitutional attack to the extent litigation occurred.[139]

Few of these loosely drawn statutes have been challenged in the Supreme Court. Statutes that were challenged have survived the kind of attack that prevailed in *Schechter*. Though, as has been indicated, no such law emcompassed an area so vast as the N.I.R.A., a number of the statutes were broad indeed. Only in controversies involving First Amendment and other personal freedom issues has the Court given more strict review.

A number of commentators have expressed the view that the *Schechter* doctrine possesses little vitality and its application would be restricted to situations involving delegations to private parties or criminal prosecutions.[140] Others—including Professor Emeritus Maurice H. Merrill of the University of Oklahoma Law Center, whose 1968 article, in the University of Nebraska Law Review, *Standards—A Safeguard for the Exercise of Delegated Power,* may be the most notable example of this view and provides useful classifications of the decisions—are equally firm in the belief that the N.I.R.A. would meet the same fate today in its enacted form.[141]

A Supreme Court decision in 1974, which expressly gave a narrow construction to a statute to avoid a constitutional separation of powers issue, supports the latter belief. The issue was one of delegation of legislative power, raised by the use of the statutory standard, "public policy or interest served," in an appropriation act that directed federal administrative agencies to impose license fees on persons regulated by them. *National Cable Television Ass'n., Inc., v. Federal Communications Commission*[142] gives some assurance that the *Schechter* doctrine remains the rule of the Court.

The decision involved a license fee imposed by the FCC upon a cable company under authority of the Independent Offices Appropriation Act, 1952, 31 USCS § 483a, which provided (the words of the statute that troubled the Court being emphasized):

> It is the sense of the Congress that any work, service. . . benefit, license . . . or similar thing of value or utility performed, furnished, provided, granted . . . by any federal agency . . . to or for any person (including . . . corporations . . .) . . . shall be self-sustaining to the full extent possible, and the head of each Federal agency is authorized by regulation . . . to prescribe therefor . . . such fee, charge, or price, if any, as he shall determine . . . to be fair and equitable taking into consideration direct and indirect cost to the Government, value to the recipient, *public policy or interest served*, and other pertinent facts. . . .

The majority opinion, written by Mr. Justice Douglas, wrote the words "public policy or interest served" out of the statute, insofar as attributing to them an independent discretionary purpose or force is concerned. The Court upheld the statute by confining the breadth of the words "public policy or interest served"—a vague, standardless term—to those charges determined to be fair and equitable after taking into consideration those direct and indirect costs to the government that are of value to the recipient. Had the vague term been given independent meaning, each agency would have been required to attach a subjective positive or negative value to the public policy or public interest being served by the person regulated. A grant of this kind of undefined discretion could invalidate the statute, under the *Schechter* decision, as a delegation of uncanalized power. As most people are aware, the Court will avoid deciding constitutional issues if possible, and it chose to do so here by the device of statutory narrowing.

The Court majority reaffirmed the *Schechter* principle that

> Congress is not permitted to abdicate or to transfer to others the essential legislative functions with which it is thus [constitutionally] vested . . .

and the *Hampton* rule that

If Congress shall lay down by legislative act an intelligible principle to which the person or body authorized to fix such rates is directed to conform, such legislative action is not a forbidden delegation of legislative power. . . .

The delegation in *National Cable* did not compare in breadth of subject matter with the delegation to the executive in *Schechter* of power to improve the national economy. Nevertheless the area of regulation covered was broad. The "public policy or interest served" provision applied to not one but a number of activities regulated by different agencies of government. The decision does not discuss this distinction. It questions "public policy . . . to be served" as an adequate basis for congressional delegation of legislative power.

Unfortunately, with some exceptions such as *National Cable*, the modern judicial trend has been to give lip service to the "intelligible principle" doctrine while accepting unintelligible standards in delegated legislation, cloaking acceptance in rationalizations, for example (borrowing in part from the administrative law writings[143] of the late Professor Frank Cooper of the University of Michigan Law School):

- The complexity and character of the subject matter is to be considered in determining whether there has been an unlawful delegation of legislative power.
- The nature of the problem requires that rulemaking bodies be allowed a wide discretion.
- In the interest of providing for flexibility, the legislature did not desire to lay down minutely defined standards.
- It is sometimes better if the legislature does not inhibit administrative discretion by the imposition of strict standards.
- Modern government with its complexities requires the policymaking of the expert.
- The legislature is not equipped to establish policies that will solve every future question.
- The Constitution does not require three airtight departments of government.
- The Supreme Court has declared statutory delegations unconstitutional on only two occasions.

When these types of judicial generalizations appear, we may expect delegations of legislative power to be upheld. These statements, defensible when accompanied by analytical reasoning, are too often used to bridge significant gaps in reasoning as a means of approving unconfined delegations of legislative power to the executive branch.

The legislative command of the Constitution is clear: "All legislative Powers ... shall be vested in ... a Congress ..." (Article I, Section 1); and the specific powers of Congress appear in Article I, Section 8, ending with the clause, "... To make all Laws which shall be necessary and proper for carrying into execution the foregoing Powers, and all other Powers vested by this Constitution in the Government of the United States, or in any Department or Officer thereof...."

The executive command of the Constitution conveys a different and separate function: "The executive power shall be vested in a President ..." (Article 2, Section 1) who shall "... give the Congress information on the State of the Union, and recommend to their consideration ... measures.... [H]e shall take care that the laws be faithfully executed...." (Article II, Section 3).

It would be unreasonable to interpret the Constitution as meaning that the President need only recommend a legislative proposal to Congress for Congress to rubber-stamp that recommendation into law. Yet this in effect is becoming the practice, largely by use of the kinds of rationalization devices in judicial opinions illustrated above.

In one such instance Mr. Justice Harlan dissented, in an opinion joined by Mr. Justice William O. Douglas and Mr. Justice Stewart that described the basic constitutional necessity for the *Schechter* principle:[144]

> *First*, it insures that the fundamental policy decisions in our society will be made not by an appointed official but by the body immediately responsible to the people. *Second*, it prevents judicial review from becoming merely an exercise at large by providing the courts with some measure against which to judge the official action that has been challenged....

CONSEQUENCES TO FEDERALISM

> The powers not delegated to the United States by the Constitution, nor prohibited by it to the States, are reserved to the States respectively, or to the people. (Amendment 10 to the Constitution)

The enumeration in the Constitution, of certain rights, shall not be construed to deny or disparage others retained by the people. (Amendment 9 to the Constitution)

Chapter 3 deals with the concern of the Founding Fathers that the Constitution of 1789 (the year of its ratification by the people) should not authorize federal encroachment upon the local concerns of the states, and illustrations appear in Chapter 2 of unduly broad statutory powers vested in federal administrators permitting intrusion into local affairs. The founders had ample cause for their concern. A leading administrative law scholar and practitioner, the late Professor Frank E. Cooper, wrote in 1964:

Whenever Congress legislates in a field in which state legislation exists, a question arises whether it will be held that the Federal legislation has preempted the field, rendering the State impotent to act therein and invalidating existing State legislation. . . .[145]

Cooper then referred to *Pennsylvania v. Nelson*, a 1956 Supreme court decision:[146]

Indicative of the unlimited potential of the preemption doctrine as a basis for striking down State legislation in a field which Congress has entered, the Court held invalid the conviction in a State Court of a reputed Communist leader on charges of sedition against the United States, because it considered that the Federal Smith Act made it clear that Congress "intended to occupy the field of sedition." The Court reached this conclusion despite the fact that the Smith Act itself specifically provided: "Nothing in this title shall be held to take away or impair the jurisdiction of the Courts of the several States under the law thereof. . . ."[147]

Professor Maurice H. Merrill, a well-known constitutional as well as administrative law scholar, expressed a similar concern for the erosion of the doctrine of federalism in an article published in the Oklahoma Law Review in 1976 entitled *How to Lose a Federal Republic without Even Half Trying*.[148]

Federal preemption of state laws even occurs through administrative orders, rules, and regulations that have no clear basis in a federal statute. This is understandable when a federal statute, in a federal sphere of action, clearly grants that kind of superseding power to the executive. But if this is not the case, and the delegation of power to the executive is in the most general and indefinite language, there should be no federal preemption.

However, the Supreme Court in *Thorpe v. Housing Authority of Durham* in 1967[149] reversed a state court eviction order which had been handed down after notice to the tenant to quit the premises and a due process hearing in the court. The eviction was ordered from a state public housing agency's project, which was financed through rent collections, local real estate tax exemption, and federal contributions. The state supreme court affirmed but granted a stay of the trial court's order pending application for certiorari to the Supreme Court of the United States. While this appeal was pending the federal Housing and Urban Development Department issued a retroactive circular requiring state agencies that owned HUD-aided projects, before giving notices of eviction, to tell the tenants the reasons in a private conference and give them an opportunity to reply or explain—a procedure not available as of right to other citizens except in the trial court proceeding. The circular also required local housing authorities to maintain future records for federal inspection summarizing the reasons for all evictions and the explanations made by the tenants. The Supreme Court held that this circular controlled and preempted state law, so it vacated the judgment of the state supreme court and remanded the case for further proceedings, twenty months after the local housing authority gave its first notice to terminate tenancy.

There is no provision for federal preemption in the federal (HUD) statute, with respect to eviction of tenants from low-rent housing, which is constructed under state enabling legislation and publicized as a local program. The HUD statute, described in Chapter 2, is one of many congressional enactments giving superficial recognition to federalism while delegating subjective contractual powers to agencies of the federal government. The federal administrator can construe the power as he desires, and can preempt state law in the process. The lengthy forms of contracts that the local housing authority must sign to secure assistance require federal approval of nearly every detail of the operation. The approval power, based on such contractual terms as "to the satisfaction of" the government, is broadly discretionary (as is the statute; see Chapter 2), thus preempting local responsibility. A breakdown in federalism results from congressional delegation of indefinite or subjective powers.

SUMMARY

We can draw from the authorities and decisions discussed only these general propositions. A statute should state an intelligible principle if it delegates a quasi-legislative power to an administrator, thereby guiding him, aiding the court on review, and, most important of all, enacting a law rather than delegating power to make the law. Whether such an intelligible principle has been stated in the law has become almost impossible to determine before a court has spoken, because the criteria the courts use to decide this question ofttimes are no firmer than the legislative standards they are examining. Less and less attention is given the words of Chief Justice William Taft,[150] that one of the chief purposes of the Convention was to separate the legislative from the executive functions, since their union under the Confederation "had not worked well."

Frequently, however, when the Court sustains statutory language that seems too indefinite to meet its own test given above, it does so only after it has searched the legislative history, its own past decisions, other parts of the statute, or past administrative practice that the court assumes the Congress intended to adopt as the missing standard in the statute. By this search the court finds the requisite firmness and clarity of statutory standards which are not apparent on the face of the statute.

However, some decisions will not bear out this latter analysis. These are not confined to wartime and foreign affairs legislation, which the Court has greeted most sympathetically and in which areas the President and the Congress have partially concurrent roles over the subject matter under specific provisions of the Constitution. Such decisions likewise occur in other areas of national concern. A reason may be the natural reluctance of the Court to strike down laws of importance, of apparent pressing need. One suspects the reason is that the Court is impressed with the necessity put upon it by the government for public action and persuaded by abundantly expressed opinion that Congress is not capable of properly defining in a law the basic legislative policies to direct such public action. In any event the result in some instances is to permit the legislative power to be delegated in a manner contrary to the intention of the Founding Fathers as reflected in the Constitution.

James Madison is only one among the eminent authorities who may be cited for the principle that our federal Constitution embodies the notion of separation of powers. He stated on the floor of the House of Representatives in the First Congress that, "If there is a principle in our Constitution, indeed in any free constitution, more sacred than another, it is just that it separates the legislative, executive and judicial powers."[151]

Thomas Jefferson's allegiance to the doctrine of separation of powers remained constant.[152]

The counsel for a subcommittee of the U.S. Senate stated recently:

> As Justice Jackson said: "With all its defects, delays, and inconveniences, men have discovered no technique for long preserving free government except that the Executive be under the law, and that the law be made by parliamentary deliberations."

> Unfortunately, in the case of most agencies, Congress has not made law. "The public interest," "reasonable rates,"—this is not law-making but abdication of law-making.[153]

The doctrine of separation of powers, and particularly its correlative, the prohibition against delegation by Congress of the lawmaking power to another branch of government, is expressly recognized by the Supreme Court of the United States. The Court a number of times has referred to the fact that the framers of the Constitution conceived this doctrine to be that which was espoused in the writings of Baron de Montesquieu.[154] Surely an indispensable part of that doctrine is that rules of conduct to be prescribed for the future as a matter of national policy may only be prescribed by Congress, the duly elected representatives of the people.

The judicially developed doctrine that legislative power may not be delegated had its origin in the principle of agency law that, due to the trust relationship between the principal and his agent, the authority delegated by the principal may not be redelegated by the agent.[155] Professor Louis Jaffe describes the doctrine in this way:[156]

> [T]he judges have, I think, merely seized on a convenient legal formula to express the underlying thought of Locke that "The Legislature neither must nor can transfer the power of making laws to anybody else, or place it anywhere but where the people have."

Today in many statutory delegations, Congress is going no further (if as far) in enacting "standards" than to follow one of the definitions of a standard that Jaffe[157] has mentioned, namely:

> The test of an adequate standard ... is ... [w]hether the definition sufficiently marks the field within which the administrator is to act so that it may be known whether he has kept within it in compliance with "the legislative will." This is Taft's (*Mahler v. Eby*) "intelligible principle" in terms of judicial control.

It is clear why a reviewing court should desire at least this clue to legislative policy, in order that the court can carry out its own required review of the statute. But the resolution of the question of improper delegation involves broader consideration than the Court's needs—for example, whether the legislature has adequately stated its will.

In February 1973, Mr. Justice Douglas, writing a dissenting opinion in which the Chief Justice, Mr. Justice Powell, and Mr. Justice Rehnquist concurred, referred approvingly to language of Mr. Justice Holmes that "it must be remembered that legislatures are ultimate guardians of the liberties and welfare of the people in quite as great a degree as the court."[158] Mr. Justice Douglas further said:

> It is easy in these insulated chambers to put an attractive gloss on an Act of Congress if five votes can be obtained. At times the legislative history of a measure is so clouded or obscure that we must perforce give some meaning to vague words. But where, as here, the consensus of the House is so clear, we should carry out its purpose no matter how distasteful or undesirable that policy may be to us, unless of course the Act oversteps constitutional boundaries.

Recognizing the state of vagueness and uncertainty, in case law application, of the doctrines of separation of powers, nondelegability of legislative power, and due process as they affect the field of this study, we have a clear need to focus upon the operation of the congressional process. We may then better appreciate whether the legislative body is, in fact, not capable of performing its primary function, or whether this is a makeweight argument conveniently at hand for use by administrators or pressure groups for the objective of obtaining utmost flexibility and expedition of action. Thus the next chapter will describe how the legislative procedure of Congress operates now.

Chapter 5

THE LEGISLATIVE PROCESS

Legislation most frequently begins in the executive branch insofar as the drafting process is concerned. The first part of this chapter describes the preparation of legislative proposals, which are actually drafts of bills, in that branch. The procedure in Congress is summarized in the next section, which also deals with the existing congressional staff aids and with efforts Congress has made in the past to curb arbitrary administrative exercise of power under laws that delegated discretion too generally.

INITIATION OF LEGISLATION IN THE ADMINISTRATIVE BRANCH

Most of the legislation enacted by Congress is proposed in the first instance either by the executive branch, or by independent administrative agencies or regulatory boards and commissions,[159] after clearance with the Office of Management and Budget. This Office is responsible to the President for determining in advance that any requested legislation is consistent with the administration's budget and program. Such legislative proposals of the administrative branch nearly always come to Congress in the form of drafts of bills, ready for introduction, and they are accompanied by statements of justification, usually of a general nature.

The departments and administrative agencies generally follow similar internal procedures in preparing proposals for grants of statutory authority from Congress.[160] A legislative section, usually within the Office of General Counsel of the department, drafts legislative proposals for introduction in Congress. The decision that legislation should be secured is made by an administrative official, perhaps upon recommendation of the general counsel, though not necessarily.

The work of drafting the proposal is performed by attorneys. Frequently they consult with technical staff persons and/or persons in policymaking positions. The draft of a bill is approved, usually without change, by the department head. It is then transmitted with a written explanation to the Director of the Office of Management and Budget. If the proposal is found to be in conformity with the program of the President—a finding that principally, although not exclusively, involves budget considerations—the department or agency is authorized to transmit the proposal to Congress.[161] When expedition is required the Office of Management and Budget may assent on the basis of oral communications or authorize transmittal to Congress with an explanation by the agency that time has not permitted clearance with the Office of Management and Budget.

Rarely does this procedure take account of the problems dealt with in this study. Professional and technical care are given to developing a draft of a bill that, if enacted, will contain the authority wanted, and to preparing a brief explanation of why the bill is needed. Seldom is thought given to inserting definitive policies and standards in the proposed bill. These, when considered, reflect only the objective of obtaining adequate authority from Congress to carry out plans of the administrator. The responsibility of Congress to provide clear legislative policy is another matter, one for Congress to protect as the concerned branch. If a member of the administrative staff should raise the question, that individual may expect the ready dispositive reply: nondelegation of legislative power is an outmoded legal concept today. "Public interest" terminology is presumed sufficient to withstand constitutional attack. The more specific the powers delegated by a statute, the greater will be the curbs on flexibility of administration, is the well-founded belief. Unlimited authority is equated with freedom and swiftness of administrative action: "getting things done." Of a certainty, it is a good deal easier and quicker to draft a "program" in general language, and more difficult and time-consuming to be specific.

These legislative proposals (for example, putting the government into new fields of activity or amending existing laws) originating with officials who will execute them if enacted are drafted in such manner as the officials believe is necessary or desirable to deal with a problem. They are drafted without special attention to the inroads the law will make upon congressional powers. That is not the drafters' problem; administrative flexibility of action ordinarily is sought, and in this sense the executive and regulatory officials, and their attorneys who undertake the drafting of the proposals as their agents, are special pleaders. Their interests and those of Congress can and do clash when the administrative advantages of a flexible statute are weighed in the balance with the legislature's constitutional responsibility to enact the laws. Congress recently gave statutory recognition to this fact by establishing an Office of Legal Counsel, discussed in the next section.

The Office of Management and Budget, Executive Office of the President, is not organized to correct this lack of balance. It has a material interest, since a proposal that forms a part of the President's program should be presented in a form that does not invite either constitutional attack or ambiguous construction (and in this way can be more efficiently administered by civil servants who look to the statutes for guidance), defeating the enforcement of a vital part of the administration's program. However, this has not been the Office of Management and Budget's view of its role, perhaps because it has not wished to risk becoming a bottleneck between agencies and Congress.

THE PROCESS IN CONGRESS

Does Congress have the tools to enact statutes that declare policy in an understandable and reasonably clear manner? The question first requires an appraisal of what its legislative workload is like, what procedures it follows, the staff it has provided itself with, and the extent to which it has drawn upon that staff for assistance on the matter at hand. This is not to overlook the necessity of Congress itself placing a priority on this subject.

Many hundreds of bills are introduced in both Senate and House at each session. A measure introduced is referred by the President of the Senate, or Speaker of the House, to a committee that has jurisdiction over the subject matter. A number of standing committees in each house of Congress have responsibility over defined areas of federal interest.

The program of legislative priorities of the chairman of a committee largely determines the extent to which the committee gives serious consideration to a particular bill, and to which the staff does so. Proposals receiving substantial attention include those made by administrative agencies with which the particular committee is concerned. Other elements of priority are the amount of interest shown among legislators for the proposed action, the extent of public interest in the subject reflected by constituents of various members of Congress, and whether the committee or subcommittee has previously investigated the subject at some length and believes that a law is needed.

Groups sometimes referred to as "pressure groups" are usually organizations having a legitimate interest in legislative proposals, such as labor, industry, municipalities, and the growing number of citizen and consumer organizations of different kinds. Such groups often constitute a significant voice in achieving active consideration for a referred bill.[162]

Most measures referred to a committee (exclusive of those introduced by a member at the request of the executive branch) are merely filed. This is usually the case unless the committee staff becomes aware that one of the factors indicated above is present and that the bill should receive active consideration. Many bills that are introduced and referred to a committee may involve the affairs of some government agency, and these are usually referred to the administrative tribunal concerned for formal comment to the committee. In such cases, the committee expects the agency to study the proposal and submit its comments to the committee after first clearing them with the executive Office of Management and Budget and further reporting to the committee whether that office is of the view that the passage of the measure would or would not be in accordance with the program of the President. In consultation with the staff, the chairman then recommends to the committee whether public hearings should be held on certain bills. The determining factors in this regard are usually whether the bill is sufficiently important and sometimes whether it is controversial. Bills that are prepared on the initiative of the executive branch and administrative agencies and introduced under sponsorship of members of either house of Congress presumably fall into the active class of bills.

The existing legislative process involves several stages after the introduction of bills, the first of which is reference of the measures to committees of the houses. Hearings are then held by subcommittees on those bills that attract sufficient interest, followed by the issuance of subcommittee and committee reports that are distributed with the legislative proposals for consideration by the house affected. These reports must be cleared for floor discussion and, in the case of the House, consideration and vote by the Rules Committee, which fixes the calendar priority of the bills. If floor debate results in adoption of a bill by either body, which does not occur often without some revision of its provisions, more particularly in the Senate, the proposed legislation is dispatched to the other body where the process follows similar lines.

The Committee Process

According to law, committee meetings are held weekly, biweekly, or monthly. They are open to the public, except that closed sessions may be held for marking up (revising) bills or for voting or when a majority so orders.[163] Hearings by a standing or special committee must be open to the public unless testimony may relate to national security or may tend to affect adversely the character or reputation of a witness or any individual or may divulge a confidential matter; open hearings involving these types of testimony are prohibited by law or regulation.[164] The statute requires at least one week's advance notice of the date, place, and subject matter of a public hearing unless a good cause is found to hold the hearing at an earlier time. Open hearings may be broadcast under such rules as a committee adopts.

At the beginning of the hearing, the chairman ordinarily reads the bill into the record and gives a brief introductory statement. The ranking minority member normally does likewise. The first witness is called. Legislators who wish to be heard usually testify first. Then witnesses for the administrative branch are heard, followed by other witnesses called by the chairman. At times administration witnesses may be invited to appear last or to testify again, after the committee has received the other testimony. If the administrative agency has no interest in the bill it may be permitted simply to file the written comments referred to earlier.

If the bill relates to the functions of a subcommittee the hearing may take place before the latter, in which event similar procedure is followed. The committee must require a witness to file a written statement of his testimony one day before his appearance, unless good cause is shown for not doing so. The law requires that the staff must prepare a summary of the testimony at the end of each hearing day for use of committee members before each day of hearing, if requested by the chairman and ranking minority member; and such summary may be printed as part of the hearings if they are ordered to be printed. The minority can also require the chairman to call witnesses they select for at least one day of hearing.

Each standing, select, or special committee of the Senate shall adopt rules governing the procedure of the committee to be published in the Congressional Record and to be consistent with the standing rules of the Senate. Each Senate committee is given statutory powers to hold hearings, subpoena witnesses and records, investigate, report hearings, employ stenographic assistance, and expend sums up to $10,000 as it deems advisable in the discharge of its functions. The chairman begins the questioning of each witness. He then gives to committee members the opportunity of questioning, alternating between parties and starting with the highest-ranking members. Testimony usually is not sworn, although it may be; it is more apt to be sworn if the hearing is of an investigative nature. Attorneys may testify and may accompany clients, but may not represent their clients in the same manner, if their clients are witnesses, as they might in the trial of a case or in an adjudicatory hearing; that is, counsel may not as a matter of right present arguments to the legislators or question or cross-examine persons testifying. The prepared statements of the witnesses are available to all committee members.

Willfully failing to testify or to produce papers when called upon to do so constitutes a misdemeanor. The penalty is a jail sentence of from one to twelve months and a fine in the minimum amount of $100 and the maximum amount of $1,000. That a witness's testimony or the production of his records may tend to disgrace him or otherwise render him infamous does not excuse such failure. In the event of his refusal, the committee may vote to bring to either house, or if Congress is out of session to the presiding officer, a certificate of failure to testify, such certificate containing a statement of facts under the seal of the Senate or House and addressed to the U.S. Attorney, requesting him to bring this matter before the Grand Jury for action.

By means of the evidence presented at the hearings, the committee members, who may not have been especially acquainted with its subject matter or its perhaps complicated or vague provisions earlier, become increasingly aware of the scope and purport of the legislative proposal. Their awareness is further increased by the opportunity to question witnesses and requestion them, often pressing a question upon witness after witness, thus becoming better informed not only regarding the content of the bill but also concerning the objections thereto and any legal and policy question that may arise. Further, they may bring their own independent judgment to bear upon the kind of legislative policy the administrative agency has drafted and requested Congress to enact into law. The hearing thus offers the committee members an opportunity to make certain that the subject matter is covered appropriately, that the provisions respecting it are sufficiently specific, and that the policies as drafted represent the committee's views. They may do this in the following ways.

If the provisions of the bill are broad and ambiguous, the members have the opportunity of impressing upon government witnesses as they testify the need to state the policy intended more specifically in order to give the congressional members an opportunity to concur or not to concur in the proposals. They may also request them, if it is found necessary, to draft revised language meeting their objections as to indefiniteness that would result in grants of excessively sweeping powers and discretion.

This is the ideal way in which a bill should be processed, but one that infrequently achieves reality largely because of committee failure to convey to the staff its interest in more definite legislative standards (as will later appear), because of lack of attendance of members at sessions or length, and because of complexity of sections and clauses, which are detailed in every way except for statements of standards and policies and which frequently exceed one hundred pages in their printed form. The committee also, through its chairman or its members, could (if the bill confers the kind of broad powers with which this study is concerned, that is, the kind exemplified in Chapter 2), ask the government witness to be prepared to testify as to how the bill will operate in practice if enacted. Also, it can ask each nongovernment witness to give his opinion on the same question and on the question of whether the government testimony showing how the bill will operate raises serious questions making further legislative redefinition necessary or desirable, and if so what solution the witness suggests by way of redrafts of provisions. This request may be made even in the notice of hearing, affording the witness more adequate time to consider the matter. All of these provisions should aid the committee at the hearing to obtain expert evidence as to how the objectives stated in the bill may be achieved through the process of sharpening and redefining all the questions relating to the how, what, and why of the legislation proposed. This technique has been used effectively by former Senator John Pastore (D., R.I.) and former Congressman Del Clawson (R., Cal.).

Members of Congress have been elected and reelected in good part because of their acumen and decisiveness in forming and making political judgments. By availing themselves of the opportunity in the hearing to become acquainted more fully with proposed legislation, to analyze the proposals made, and to cross-question those especially concerned with the proposals, they place themselves in a position to make the kind of decisions necessary in order to determine whether a law should be enacted and in what form—political decisions they are exceptionally qualified to make. If they find that at the end of the hearings the scope of the legislation is unclear in certain major or minor respects, the members or the chairman may request witnesses to file in writing, within a fixed time after testifying or after the hearing ends, their explanation or understanding of the revised drafts, particularly of any vague or ambiguous provisions. This would enable the committee to clarify and illustrate the intent of the law proposed by redrafting the measure or by exposition and construction of ambiguous language in committee reports that are filed.

That remains for the most part an abstraction, convertible into practice only if the legislators receive sufficient information from their committee staffs and their specialized drafting staff (Office of Legislative Counsel), later described. This contingency likewise requires adequate personnel to carry into execution valuable suggestions developed in committee hearings, by researching, drafting, and translating them into valid, workable legislative solutions. It also involves integrating the Legislative Counsel's Office, described below, into the legislative process as an integral part of congressional consideration on all active bills, or (with the same objective in mind) establishing a similar internal office for the special purpose of bringing to the attention of Congress and assisting Congress to resolve separation of powers problems in bills under active committee consideration, most particularly problems of delegation of legislative power to agencies created to execute laws.

Committee Reports

A stenographic record is made of each hearing and furnished to the committee members as soon as possible. At a convenient time after the transcript of the hearing becomes available in printed form, the committee is called into executive session. The measure or measures on which hearings were held are considered and approved, or the members may revise the bill, or it may receive a "do not pass" recommendation. If the hearing was held by a subcommittee the same procedure is followed but a report is given to the standing committee of "favorable for passage" or "to table" the bill. A favorable report no doubt will be accompanied by certain recommended changes made in the mark-up session that would constitute amendments to the bill as considered in committee. The subcommittee report is then considered at a meeting of the standing committee, whose recommendation is accompanied by a written committee report that would state the purpose, scope, and reasons for favoring the bill if passage is recommended. Changes in existing laws and the text of laws repealed must be set out under House rule.[165]

Committee reports on measures that are approved for passage must be filed promptly with the Senate,[166] a majority of members being required to be present for such action. Members of the committee have three days from the date of their request, if timely made, to file supplemental, minority, or additional views with the majority report. A measure reported by a standing committee of the Senate cannot be considered by the Senate unless the report is available to the members of the Senate at least three calendar days prior to consideration by that body; and if a hearing was held, the committee is required to make a reasonable effort to have the hearing transcript available for distribution at that time.

Such reports provide an efficient means of clarifying policy and intent if these are expressed too broadly or unclearly in the bill. Here the committee can explain as definitely as possible how the objectives of the measure, if expressed in phrases that may be obscure—such as the "public interest" or the "public welfare"—are to be applied, and in what manner, to whom, why, and under what general conditions and circumstances; further, what the basic duties and powers of the agency executing the law shall be. It can restrict excessive discretion in its implementation by using the word "shall" and not "may" when feasible, thus preventing an administrative construction that the executive has the option of deciding when to apply or not to apply the law. This kind of clarification of intent and purpose by committee report forms the best evidence of legislative history of a law that can be found. It is suggested that each report might easily, by House rules, be required to include a special section devoted to stating the definitive policy intended by any particular language that in the committee's view may be subject to conflicting interpretation.

Floor Consideration

In the House, once given a favorable committee report, a bill is assigned a Union or House calendar number and, if it is uncontroversial, is placed on the consent calendar. However, if it is a controversial bill, it is taken up in order except for the need for a special "rule" from the House Committee on Rules as a condition to consideration by the full body.[167]

A further source of legislative history for the purpose of clarifying a vague statutory provision is the record of debate in either house, notably when the sponsor and floor leader of the measure, speaking on behalf of the committee, explains the provisions of the bill and answers questions raised by the members in relation to the measure.

If the bill passes one House, it is engrossed and sent with a message to the other; the presiding officer refers it to a standing committee, and the same procedure is followed as in the first House. In the Senate no distinction is made between bills raising revenue, or making appropriations, and other bills. After passage of the bill by the second House it is reported back to the originating body, and concurrence is requested in any amendments that have been affixed by the former.

Conference of the Two Houses

If the amendments are minor, the standing committee of the originating House can recommend unanimous agreement with such amendments and have the matter put to the assembly for a majority vote. If the amendments are considered substantial or controversial, the initiating body may vote to request a conference. If so, the Speaker or President pro tem, depending upon the House involved, appoints conferees called managers. They can be from both parties or from only one. They are sometimes referred to as the "Third House of Congress."[168] The authority of the conferees is limited to consideration of the amendments. The conferees upon reaching agreement must issue a report, which can include only matters germane to subjects in disagreement between the two bodies. This is true by statute regarding the Senate. Usually a compromise results in conference. If a stalemate occurs, new conferees may be appointed as a remedy. A House can instruct its conferees, but this is rare. The conferees have no power to file a minority report; the conference report must come in the form of a majority recommendation. A statement explaining the effect of amendments recommended must be attached.

The conference report offers a final means of obtaining legislative history to clarify the meaning of indefinite or obscure language in legislation. It is one of the sources of statutory interpretation and thus affords a means for explaining congressional intent otherwise stated only vaguely in the bill.

The White House

When a measure has passed both Houses it is enrolled in the House that originated the legislation. Thereafter the clerk of the Subcommittee on Enrolled Bills delivers the completed bill to the White House. The White House refers a copy of the bill to the departments or other administrative agencies concerned, as well as the Attorney General, for advice, and the President makes his determination whether to approve or veto the legislation. At this point, a separation of powers question also can be raised by the President's message, though it would not be effective unless the message was accompanied by a veto.

Staff Aids

Committee Staff

As indicated earlier, each committee is equipped with a staff, the size of which may vary greatly, headed by a chief clerk or counsel. Staff members of the committee or subcommittee play an active role, and they discuss the measure informally with officials or staff of the executive branch or administrative agency to an extent depending upon such factors as whether the administration in power is of the same political party, the amount of sympathetic interest the committee chairman takes in the proposal, and how open and cordial the staff relationships are. The line of authority of the subcommittee's staff is to the chairman, who may or may not make their analyses and recommendations available to other subcommittee members. The line of authority from the subcommittee is to the full committee, and the committee's staff likewise may advise on an informal rather than formal basis, with no uniform pattern regarding the kind of advice required or sought.

Office of Legislative Counsel

Legislative drafting experts are provided for by statute and are known as Senate and House Legislative Counsel. The committees (and, in the House, the members as well) may turn to these experts for assistance in writing clear policy directives into legislation.

An Office of Legislative Counsel[169] was created in each House by statute, to be under the direction of an attorney who is chiefly required to give aid in drafting public bills and resolutions or amendments on the request of any committee of either House.

The Legislative Counsel in the House is appointed by the Speaker and serves at the pleasure of the Speaker. He may appoint such attorneys as he needs, one of whom the Legislative Counsel shall designate as Deputy Legislative Counsel. The provisions relating to the Office of Senate Legislative Counsel are similar, except that appointment of the Legislative Counsel is made by the President pro tempore of the Senate; the Committee on Rules and Administration may determine which committee shall receive preference in requests for aid in drafting public bills and resolutions or amendments thereto. Effective October 1, 1978, the number of employees in the Office of Legislative Counsel of the Senate who may be designated as senior counsel was increased to five. Periodic increases have enlarged the number of attorneys in the Senate Legislative Counsel's Office by 1985 to seventeen, and in the Office of Legislative Counsel of the House of Representatives to thirty-five. The difference in staffing clearly has a basis in the relatively large number of representatives who can call upon the office, as compared with the number of members in the other body.

The technical difficulties involved and skills required in such staff analysis and draftsmanship were stated at the time of the creation of the Office as follows:[170]

> The law is or should be treated as a science. The Office of the Legislative Counsel, devoted in the widest sense to expert draftmanship, is designed to represent that ideal and to arrest, as far as possible, the tendency more or less due to the pressure of circumstances, to prolixity, disorder and uncertainty in statutory enactments.

> The preparation of an act of legislation may present various phases, each of which involves a distinct problem. First, there must be a definite purpose or intention; but this is not as simple as it sounds. . . . Secondly, the subject matter, instead of being single or simple, may be highly complicated and require the consideration, adjustment and reconciliation of numerous elements. In the third place, it is necessary to bear in mind the machinery already provided for the application and enforcement of the proposed measure and the possible necessity of prescribing administrative details. Fourthly, the new measure should be examined in connection with any previous legislation on the same subject or on similar subjects, and not merely with the text of such legislation but also with pertinent judicial and administrative interpretations.

It was said also:[171]

> In all matters of drafting, knowledge of constitutional and ad-
> ministrative law is invaluable. . . . The relations between the
> three branches of government, so far as prescribed by the Con-
> stitution, are very commonly involved in matters of legislation.
> Again, most of the complex legislative problems today involve
> extensive executive machinery for enforcement and ad-
> ministration. In the legislative provision for this machinery
> there must be met the many administrative and constitutional
> law problems involved in the form in which the executive ac-
> tion may properly express itself and in the judicial review of
> such action. . . .

It should be emphasized that it is the responsibility of these offices to
serve only when called upon. They serve only upon request or invitation.
No law or rule says that the request or invitation must be extended. In
other words, important and novel legislation may, and probably more
often than not does, travel its route through the legislative process with
no review by either office, valuable though such review would be, and
relevant as that review could also be to the problems discussed in several
of these chapters if counsel were apprised of leadership interest in providing for more definitive standards to guide administrative discretion in
each bill reviewed.

The existing Office of Legislative Counsel is now called upon to a
limited extent to review drafts of particular bills prepared in executive
agencies, but with no regularity. Situations may occur in which the Chief
Executive requests Congress to authorize the administration to carry out
an objective it has in mind but has not reduced to a written legislative
proposal. In such case the Legislative Counsel's Office will probably be
requested to draft the desired measure. The professional caliber of this
office his high, but its assistance is customarily requested for reasons irrelevant to this study, such as a congressional request for draft of a new
law or an amendment to a present statute—needs that the executive agency itself fills on legislation in which it has an interest. The order of
preference that has been in effect for many years is the following: (1)
measures in conference between the two Houses; (2) measures pending on
the floor of the Senate; (3) measures pending before a standing committee; and (4) original measures being prepared for individual members of
the Senate. The office has no part in the formulation of the legislative

policy. It should, however, have a significant concern with policy. That is, it should ascertain the desired policy in adequate detail *and with sufficient precision* to enable it to formulate a measure that is technically effective to carry out legislative intent. It is clear that the words "technically effective" do not require the office to consider issues of separation of powers and excessive delegation of power that may be raised by the bill being drafted. However, this would not prevent the Senate from charging the office with responsibility to undertake this additional duty.

The statute relating to the Legislative Counsel in the House of Representatives provides: ". . . the purpose of the Office is to advise and assist the House . . . and its committees and Members, in the achievement of a clear, faithful, and coherent expression of legislative policies. . . ."[172] The kind of descriptive words following "achievement" in this statutory provision are not used in the earlier Senate statute. Nevertheless it appears that both offices have always performed the function that is now a part of the charter of House Legislative Counsel.

During the Ninetieth Congress approximately forty-five hundred measures were drafted by the Office. However, almost none of these were the kind of bill that delegates discretionary powers to administrative agencies. Of greater significance is the number of new subjects of federal legislation of the latter type that has occupied the attention of Congress during that period, and the increasing technical complexity of many of those subjects.

Although the office is required by the statute that created it to render service only to committees, it has long been its practice to furnish drafting service also to individual members of the Senate on their request to the extent permitted by its personnel strength.

Service rendered to a standing committee with respect to a single measure may include assistance to subcommittee staff members in the preparation of amendments required to carry into effect policy decisions made from time to time by the subcommittee during its consideration of the measure, and in the preparation of the amended measure for reporting to the full committee. It may include similar assistance to members of the staff of the full committee before the measure is reported for floor action. Assistance also may be given in the preparation of any floor amendments requested on behalf of the member in charge of the measure on the floor. In the case of a measure as to which a conference is requested to resolve differences between the Senate and the House of Representatives, assistance may be furnished in the preparation of the conference report. Members of the office are consulted often by members of the staffs of committees and subcommittees and by members of the staffs of individual senators. Such consultation occurs with respect to possible approaches to the legislative solutions of particular problems, technical questions of substantive and procedural law, and such matters as the mechanics of the preparation of reports, the technical legal accuracy of reports, and fulfillment of the requirements of the Cordon Rule.

Effective drafting requires careful analysis of the legal problems involved, arrangement of matter in a logical sequence, and accurate and unambiguous expression of the concepts set forth. Constitutional limitations must always be observed. Most legislative proposals deal with matters that have been the subject of one or more previous enactments. A new measure must be carefully related to earlier enactments to produce, as far as possible, a consistent body of law that will carry the congressional purpose into effect without producing unintended consequences.

However, the law (and common practice) leaves it completely discretionary with the committee whether to call upon these legislative specialists. Accordingly, on much, if not most, important legislation their proficiency is not utilized. Since use of this technical skill is almost essential in order to determine whether undue discretionary power is being delegated to an administrative tribunal in a particular bill, the fact that it is not adequately called upon is a present defect of the legislative process, but one that can easily be remedied. When it is utilized the result will also be to enable legislators to form a better judgment upon how to cast their votes on a bill, based upon the fuller understanding that will be provided by a statement of policies and standards in the legislation. As noted earlier, the Constitution provides that "[a]ll legislative powers herein granted shall be vested in a Congress of the United States, which shall consist of a Senate and a House of Representatives."

Office of Senate Legal Counsel

As a part of the Ethics in Government Act in 1978, Congress established the Office of Senate Legal Counsel. The original proposal by the Senate was to establish a joint House-Senate Office of Congressional Legal Counsel, but the House was not prepared to agree to a joint office at that time. The Senate, having considered the subject for a number of years, decided to establish its own Office of Senate Legal Counsel, primarily to defend its interest in court. The Senate committee report shows that there was no intention to question the good faith of representation by the Department of Justice, and the Attorney General did not

object to the creation of the office or view it as a violation of the separation of powers concept. Not infrequently, the Attorney General (who
primarily must represent the interests of the executive) finds himself in a
conflict-of-interest situation due to departmental challenges of statutes.
And the volume of cases involving release of congressional or executive
papers and many other matters having a present or future interest to Congress was growing. The Senate felt that by establishing its own litigation
office there would be more consistent attention to issues and cases constantly arising in the courts that could substantially affect the powers of
Congress and its independent role under the separation of powers doctrine.

The statute[173] is considered, however, as referring only to litigation;
it is not intended to apply to legislative review or counseling functions
having to do with separation of powers and other constitutional issues,
presented by legislative proposals not yet enacted. Nonetheless the
statute is some evidence that Congress is acting to protect its own authority. It needs to go further and protect its jurisdiction when confronted with
legislative proposals submitted by the Executive that would delegate
legislative policy making to officials of the executive branch.

Other Staff Assistance

Congress and its committees have been equipped with other aids,
whose functions bear less directly upon the subject under discussion, but
who nevertheless on occasion may be extremely helpful. The Librarian of
Congress is authorized by statute to appoint specialists in twenty-three
broad fields for the purpose of lending their assistance through the Congressional Research Service (a separate department in the Library of Congress) to Congress and congressional committees.[174] This research department is not only authorized to give help to committees and to members
generally to evaluate legislative proposals or recommendations by the
president or an executive agency, but provision is also made for analyzing
policy areas in substance at the opening of the Congress. As has been
seen earlier, development and provision of definitive legislative policy is
at the heart of the problem under discussion. Furthermore, the staff is
authorized and directed to prepare summaries and digests of bills upon
request, and to prepare on request by a committee or a member of Congress a memorandum on any measure on which hearings have been announced. The Librarian is also authorized to maintain and develop
specialists and consultants to perform these functions. Notwithstanding

the fact that these functions are of a policy research character rather than of a constitutional and drafting nature, law and policy often are intertwined, inviting the utilization of both functions.

CURES ATTEMPTED BY CONGRESS

As we have seen, Congress has been negligent, when delegating powers to the executive branch, in failing to give clear and reasonable directions as to what it wants done. Congress has continued to fail in this way, though painfully aware, through complaints of constituents, of many examples of arbitrary enlargement or misuse of their statutory discretion by administrative officials.

Congress first attempted to meet the problem by providing for an expanded and uniform due process procedure through administrative hearings before independent hearing examiners for individuals adversely affected by government action, in the form of a Federal Administrative Procedure Act adopted in 1946.[175] This Federal Administrative Procedure Act also required public notice and opportunity to comment in writing before administration regulations (with some exceptions) could become effective, and the Act gave greater rights of judicial review. These steps were helpful in improving agency procedure, but they did not significantly contribute to resolving the central problem, which is one of substance.

Again, rather than deal with the problem directly by spelling out its purposes more precisely in the statutory delegation itself, the legislators devised a back-door method whereby they could oversee administrative exercise of discretion. The method, increasingly used in recent years, is referred to as the "congressional veto," disapproved by the Supreme Court in 1983.[176]

Jagdish Rai Chadha, an alien who was admitted to this country under a nonimmigrant student visa, remained when the visa expired. He was given a suspension of deportation hearing by the Justice Department, as provided by statute. The Justice Department thereafter ordered the deportation suspended, and the matter was reported to Congress in conformity with the Immigration Act.

The statute authorized either House of Congress, by resolution, to invalidate such a decision of the Attorney General upon report to Congress by the executive. Such resolution was adopted by the House of Representatives, vetoing the suspension. The Justice Department reopened the hearing, and Chadha moved to terminate the proceeding, challenging the constitutionality of the congressional veto resolution. After pursuing his administrative remedies without success, Chadha appealed the order of deportation.

The Supreme Court affirmed the U.S. Court of Appeals, holding that the congressional veto provision in the law was invalid in two respects: violation of the constitutional requirement of bicameralism, and violation of the requirement of the Constitution, Article I, Section 7, Clause 3, that every order, resolution, or vote to which the concurrence of both Houses was necessary (except on a question of adjournment) shall be presented to the President for approval or veto.

The House resolution disapproving the Attorney General's action was ruled legislative in character since it altered Chadha's status. Accordingly, under the bicameral provisions of the Constitution, it required action by both houses of Congress, not just one. Further, since the Presentment Clause paraphrased above requires that legislation be submitted to the President for approval or veto before taking effect, this procedure should have been followed because the resolution was legislative in nature and effect.

Thus, the U.S. Constitution sets this nation apart from countries such as Great Britain, where much the same technique as the legislative veto is used with respect to what is candidly referred to as "delegated legislation" (namely the statute-implementing rules and orders of administrative agencies that in Britain are expressly authorized by many acts of Parliament). This practice is appropriate in Britain where Parliament is supreme and there is no written constitution providing for separation of powers, somewhat unique characteristics of our national form of government, and for executive veto.

The Court's elimination of the congressional veto tool, which the legislature used to prevent the executive branch from misusing its broadly delegated authority, makes it necessary for Congress to reexamine—or truly to examine for the first time—the *source* of the problem: the administratively drafted bill.[177]

SUMMARY

The legislative process reviewed in this chapter appears adequate to the task of fashioning legislative policy. Yet it is seldom, if ever, adequately utilized insofar as the problem at hand is concerned. And this failure to use available staff and to organize these staff offices into institutional size, operating under institutional procedure, for this limited legislative function, somewhat more comparable to their administrative counterparts, may be the focus of the difficulty.[178]

The comparison, if evaluated, appears as a contrast, since every executive department, administrative agency, or independent administrative board or commission of any size in Washington has a legislative counsel and staff for drafting legislative proposals. That staff also prepares comments on proposed legislation of interest, as well as preparing administrators for congressional hearings, and so on. There is institutional imbalance when the two branches are thus compared, the legislative branch being peculiarly and overwhelmingly outbalanced in staffing for the legislative drafting function by the executive branch. This has in all likelihood had a marked effect in the indefinite delegations of executive authority that we have seen. John Austin, in his work on jurisprudence, referred to what he called the "technical" part of legislation as "imcomparably more difficult than what may be styled as the ethical. In other words, it is far easier to conceive justly what would be useful law, than so construct that same law that it may accomplish the design of the law giver."[179]

Another focal need is to add to the congressional staff experts in constitutional law or to provide them as consultants, so that members may obtain their opinions on the separation of powers, nondelegation, and due process issues discussed above. The opinions should be made a part of the bill file with respect to all legislation receiving active consideration in either House. Such opinions would be rendered upon a timely basis so that every member of Congress becomes aware (or has the opportunity to become aware) of instances of undue delegation of discretion in bills while they are in process.

Chapter 6

CONCLUSIONS AND RECOMMENDATIONS

CONCLUSIONS

The Constitution provides that Congress shall make the laws and the President shall carry them out. The Founding Fathers, as noted in Chapter 3, emphasized that no power, legislative or judicial in nature, should be delegated by Congress to the Chief Executive. And yet it has become an everyday occurrence, which we see illustrated in Chapters 2 and 4, for Congress to disregard this injunction by enacting directionless delegations of authority and function in bills prepared and presented by the executive branch.

Such was not the intention of the framers of the Constitution. This conclusion follows if we consider the nature of the powers given to each branch, chiefly in Articles I to III; the insistence upon separation of powers among the branches; and the checks and balances provided them as defensive measures. More specifically, the final clause of James Madison's motion described in Chapter 3, which would have provided an express constitutional basis for delegations by Congress to the Executive, was defeated. The Founding Fathers intended to authorize the executive to carry out and execute the laws (and to restrict the executive to that basic function). To authorize (as the last clause of Madison's motion provided) Congress also to delegate powers not legislative or judicial in nature would be redundant since Congress would be authorized thereby to delegate only administrative powers and these the executive had already received by direct grant in the Constitution. If it were not redundant (and therefore unnecessary), it would constitute an authorization to Congress to delegate to the Executive powers that the founders in their wisdom did not wish the Executive to have.

89

The obvious reason for the defeat of the clause was the foresight of the delegates to the Constitutional Convention: they clearly perceived that an attempt to define such a delegation by constitutional provision would raise more problems than it would solve. Thus had the delegation resolution been adopted it could have had an uncertain, ambiguity-creating effect upon the several powers that the Constitution distributed in Articles I, II, and III among the branches of government, and upon the provisions for checks and balances. Why open this Pandora's Box? Congress already possessed incidental power to delegate ministerial and discretionary powers to the Executive as a part of its enactments, though not legislative powers, which are irrevocably vested in Congress by express provisions of Article I that are buttressed—if such were necessary—by the constitutional separation of powers doctrine.

In the process of defeating the Madison motion, delegates expressed their views that powers either legislative or judicial in nature must not be delegated by Congress to the executive branch. Whether a statute that grants authority to an administrative agency, board, or commission is granting any power that is "legislative or judicial in nature" requires construction. For such analytical tasks the judiciary is especially equipped, as it has shown, for example, when analyzing and refusing to enforce statutory provisions that have delegated to the courts powers of an executive nature.[180] However, it has only struck down two statutory provisions as unconstitutional delegations of legislative powers to the Executive, both decisions in 1934. One dealt with statutory provisions of the "Here is the problem; deal with it" order.

The Supreme Court had held that a law delegating power to the Executive, in order to meet the requirements of the Constitution, must provide an intelligible principle that will guide and restrict the exercise of administrative discretion. However, the Court has sustained statutes that do not meet this test, rarely holding such a law unconstitutional. In the process the rights of the states, intended to be preserved by the Constitution, also disappear through administrative encroachment.

The problem is with the application of the intelligible principle test. More often than not the judicial opinions do not analyze the statutory delegation. They resort to rationalizations to achieve a result favorable to the statute. Counselors advise clients to bow to the will of the bureaucracy, there being little chance for successful appeal. Costly administrative penalties for noncompliance over a lengthy appeal period may be incurred.

A variety of reasons account for the judicial attitude. Some judges may be motivated to concur in a statutory social program they believe desirable. They may conclude that the Founding Fathers did not foresee the complexities of modern society, and accordingly the nondelegation doctrine is not applicable. Other judges may be impressed by the unsupported argument of counsel (and some legal scholars) that requiring legislative grants of discretion to administrative agencies to be enacted in more definite terms would demand the impossible of Congress and/or impede necessary administrative flexibility. A court may presume that since the government is administering the statute on a day-to-day basis its view of the statutory meaning is a more correct one. These and other characterizations lead to the common assertion that the Constitution actually is what the courts say it is.

Further, the idea that the Constitution is what the courts say it is, a "living document" that changes with the backgrounds and beliefs of individual justices, is objectionable because it misconceives the constitutional duty of the federal judiciary under Article III, merges two basic functions of government, and violates the concept of separation of powers. The Founding Fathers contented themselves with adopting "checks and balances" provisions that served the twin purpose of avoiding an unreasonable separation of the branches of government and of providing defensive weapons to each branch against encroachment by another branch. Trading off basic powers among the three branches of government finds no support in the checks and balances provisions and circumvents the doctrine of separation of powers.

That this violation of the separation of powers doctrine causes serious harm to the rights of the states as well, rights expressly preserved in the Constitution and by the Tenth Amendment, has been demonstrated. One of this country's legislative leaders, the late Senator Robert A Taft, gave the reason:

Nothing is so characteristic of totalitarian states today as the uniting of the legislative and executive functions in one man with control also over the judges. If one man can make the laws, can execute the laws, and can judge the violation of the laws, liberty cannot long exist. We may still vote once in four years, but the election becomes a mere plebiscite where the only vote is "Ja." The very essence of individual freedom is equal justice under a rule of law, a law to which every man shall be subject and which no executive can modify.[181]

To protect the rights of the people and preserve the sovereignty of the states, and concurrently to chart the course of the new federal government along paths of present and future national need, the concept of separation of powers was established as a cornerstone of continuing importance. In the words of the late renowned Harvard Law School dean, Roscoe Pound:

> We ... deduce from a written constitution and a constitutional separation of powers that the legal order must endorse the constitution as law binding all departments of government ... as against legislative, executive, or administrative action at variance with the Constitution or exceeding the powers as defined or limited. ... These ... views are not the result of logic but of history. ...[182]

That was why General Charles Pinckney, James Madison, and the other founders determined that the power to formulate legislative policy should never be delegated to members of a branch not elected by the people. Their experience with an English monarch had been too recent, and their substitution of a President was as yet an untested experiment. They would have deemed it self-evident that if the national legislature adopted a practice of enacting laws barren of meaning and policy direction, leaving these essentials to be filled in by administrators of another branch, the practice would violate the Constitution.

Failure to credit the founders with such foresight, wisdom, and intellect is to disregard historical fact. As Alexander Hamilton wrote in THE FEDERALIST PAPERS, enacted laws are supreme, but they must be made pursuant to the Constitution in order to rise to that paramount position. He said:

> A Law, by the very meaning of the term, includes supremacy. It is a rule which those to whom it is prescribed are bound to observe. ...[183]

Who would contend otherwise?

Separation of powers is sound not only for political reasons. The liberties of individuals are threatened by criminal statutes for which the ultimate sanction is imprisonment.

Most federal agency statutes, as noted in Chapter 4, provide for criminal prosecution for a violation, not only of the statute, but also of an administrative regulation promulgated in accordance with the statute. To subject citizens to imprisonment for violation of rules drafted by unelected administrators further emphasizes the necessity for enacting legislative standards to guide and control administrative authority.

The courts do not—considering the small number of administrative orders that are appealed, the delay involved in litigation, and their own lack of constitutional authority to issue advisory opinions—provide an adequate long-range remedy for ills that are caused by the inattention of Congress to the definition of legislative policy.

The practical answer is for Congress to give greater functioning responsibility to its own expert staff as a reviewing and drafting arm with respect to all legislation emanating from the Executive. It should do so for reasons analogous to those that caused the Senate recently to create an Office of Legal Counsel to guard its jurisdictional position vis a vis the Executive in pending litigation raising an apparent clash of governmental interests on the part of the two bodies. Its stronger reason, however, would be the need for sharper definition of legislative policy.

Laws delegating legislative authority are prepared by administrators who receive the delegation, as pointed out in Chapter 5. Their activities are not coordinated with those of other agencies, and the attorneys are not as a rule trained in conforming new laws to all subjects they affect in the U.S. Code. Officials write extremely flexible provisions to obtain power for every contingency, so flexible in their statement of legislative policy that statutory language is vague and indefinite, as illustrated at length in Chapter 2.

The most significant point, however, is that administration drafters may be expert in the functions of their agencies, but they have no demonstrated expertness in constitutional law respecting the jurisdiction and responsibilities of the legislative branch. When a jurisdictional question arises between the two branches, it is implicit that agency administrators have a vested interest in preserving and extending the powers delegated by the legislative branch to the executive.

Such considerations led to the recent creation by Congress of the Office of Senate Legal Counsel. This new office may not be organized to meet the need discussed in this study, namely to give consulting service to congressional committees on legislative matters. But the need exists. There is an urgent necessity to fill the congressional vacuum by using a corps of congressional staff specialists, on a regular basis, with regard to legislative proposals of the administration in order to guard against infringement of the doctrine of separation of powers.

Most of the tools for a solution exist. A procedure for making them effective requires only an Executive Order by the President, and a congressional resolution or rule by Congress. The principles embodied in the following recommendations will serve to bring about the necessary and desirable solution. It is recommended that Congress, in coordination with the executive, establish procedures as follows for both the legislative branch and the executive branch, including independent administrative agencies and regulatory boards and commissions.

RECOMMENDATIONS

Changes in the Administrative Branch

1. Circular No. A-19 of the Office of Management and Budget should be amended to effectuate these changes in the procedure for submitting administrative agencies' legislative proposals to Congress. The changes would introduce the following governmental requirements.

Any legislative proposal that the administration submits to Congress containing provisions delegating discretionary powers, duties, or functions to the administration should be accompanied by a supporting memorandum. The memorandum, in addition to explaining the background, need, and reasons for the proposal (as customary), will include the following matters. In a separate section of the supporting memorandum the administration should (a) state that the powers being delegated are provided in definite and specific language to enable objective application of legislative policy, including intelligible and definitive directions for the administrator in making discretionary determinations; and (b) identify the proposed language that supports this statement. The separate section of the memorandum also should set forth an opinion of counsel of the proposing department or administrative agency that he has examined the proposal and the foregoing requirements have been met. If he disagrees and cannot concur in such statement, he should so state and give the reason in an opinion set forth in this section.

2. An Office of Legislative Counsel should be established in the Department of Justice headed by an Assistant Attorney General. This official should review, within a two-week period from the date of reference, such legislative proposals and the statement of agency counsel before their submission to Congress. This office should be equipped with skills comparable to the Office of Legislative Counsel in Congress, referred to

in Chapter 5, and also should include attorneys expert in constitutional law. The concurring or disagreeing opinion of this office should be made a part of the above submission to Congress. Nothing in this paragraph 2 is intended to prevent informal conferences between agency counsel and the Assistant Attorney General and their staffs, held to discuss possible changes in the legislative proposal that will adequately define its policy provisions.

3. Circular No. A-19 should also be amended to direct the Office of Management and Budget to assure that the agency counsel's memorandum and Assistant Attorney General's memorandum referred to above are submitted to Congress with and as a part of the legislative proposal. Agency counsel and the Assistant Attorney General's staff should also subsequently cooperate with the appropriate staff counsel of Congress in drafting provisions for such statutory delegations to the administrative agency that fulfill the objectives of 1(a), above.

Explanatory Note

As a usual matter, in the administration the staff work would involve the bureau chief, who would administer the proposed law; the general counsel's staff, which drafts the proposal; the Office of Management and Budget; and an Office of Legislative Counsel (or of Legislative Review if preferred), which would be established in the Department of Justice. The Department of Justice has served in somewhat similar reviewing roles at intervals in the past with reference to requests for legislation on the part of certain departments of government, but rarely with reference to those of the scores of administrative and regulatory agencies not falling within cabinet departments. Moreover, the department (and the administrative agency or regulatory board or commission as well)—since it has tended in the past to reflect the administrative view that definitive standards are unnecessary in congressional delegations of power and authority under the decisions of the courts—should be made expressly aware that it is the will of Congress that legislative proposals submitted for enactment by the Administration should provide clear statements of legislative policy with respect to the administrative discretion being requested.

An example of how a somewhat similar administrative process works in practice may be helpful. The Constitution of the Federal Republic of Germany (1949), partially due to the excesses of the Hitler regime, provides for separation of powers and requires that legislation delegating power to the Executive shall state the content, scope, and purpose of the delegated powers. The Constitution also sets forth a general principle, applicable but swept aside by Hitler, that "... the executive shall be bound by law and justice ..."—which is relevant to extremely broad executive discretion. The government established the following procedure.

Every bill submitted by the Government to Parliament must first be reviewed by the Minister of Justice, and usually by the Minister of Interior as well. The Justice Ministry reviews all bills, mainly for conformity to constitutional requirements. The Ministry also reviews them for conformity to general rules regarding form, and for conformity with existing laws, questions raised by the courts, and questions of basic human rights. The Minister of Interior has been involved in constitutional review for historical reasons dating from the time of Bismarck. The review by each occurs irrespective of which department has jurisdiction over the subject matter, such as communications or highways.

In practice, the Minister affected drafts a bill, which he gives to the Minister of Justice for review. If the Minister of Justice, after review for conformity with constitutional requirements (emphatically including separation of powers) and the other tests referred to above, finds the bill satisfactory, he approves it. If the special staff of either the Ministry of Justice or the Ministry of Interior raises a constitutional question, the staff chief calls his functionary counterpart in the originating Ministry and advises him. For example, a problem of vagueness of statutory discretion to be delegated in the bill would occasion such a call. Conferences are then held between the official competent to deal with the bill and an official of the Ministry that drafted the measure.

Each bill is accompanied by an explanation that, if clear enough, may be drawn upon to supply the guidelines required to make the powers being delegated definite and intelligible. If they are not clear enough, further conferences are held by the representative of the originating department and the reviewing ministry staff member for the purpose of putting questions and receiving answers, assisting the reviewer in understanding what powers are necessary to enable the proposed program to work in practice. With this information the reviewing representative of the Ministry of Justice is able to elaborate in bill form the legislative standards for the powers to be delegated.

There are few cases in which the term "public interest" would not be criticized by the Ministry of Justice as too indefinite, though Ministry officials state that after an examination of the entire bill it might obtain clarity from other contexts.

Should the Justice and Interior departments be unable to obtain a satisfactory resolution of the questions they raise with the originating Ministry, they have a special right to object to introduction of the bill on constitutional grounds, and if the Cabinet supports their position the bill may not be introduced; however, this right is seldom exercised, conflicts being resolved in conference.

No similar staff procedure exists in the German *Parliament.*

Changes in the Legislative Branch

1. Congress should require by rule that all bills submitted as legislative proposals of the executive branch, including the administrative agencies and independent regulatory boards and commissions, be reviewed and reported upon by the Legislative Counsel of the Senate and House of Representatives or by a specially established Office of Legislative Review of the Senate or House or of Congress, for compliance with the requirement that the bills contain adequate and intelligible standards. This review and report should be made with respect to bills on which a committee or subcommittee is seriously considering taking action. If possible the report should be made prior to the holding of committee or subcommittee hearings (if any) on the bill, assuring that a report by such congresssional office would be available to the committee membership with respect to legislation under active consideration by Congress and that members of Congress are made aware of any separation of powers question presented by an Administration legislative proposal at a time conveniently in advance of floor discussion and vote.

2. The review should be assigned by congressional resolution or rule to a Congressional Office of Legislative Review established for this purpose, or to the Office of Legislative Counsel of the Senate or House of Representatives. The review should be accomplished in consultation with the counsel (and his staff) of the committee or subcommittee holding hearings upon the legislation—or, if helpful, with agency counsel or Justice Department staff. A review memorandum discussing any issues aforementioned of delegation of legislative power, together with curative changes suggested by the above counsel in the language of the bill, should be completed prior to the closing of the hearing record. Preferably, as indicated above, the memorandum should be available to legislators prior to the opening of the hearing as an aid in questioning witnesses on such issues. Notice should be given when the hearing begins,

if practicable, of any questions raised, or substantial changes in the bill suggested, in this memorandum, unless such items have been satisfactorily resolved earlier.

3. The congressional staff memorandum should, together with the memorandum of agency counsel and concurrence or separate opinion of the Legislative Review Office of the Department of Justice dealing with the delegation issue, be made a specially identified part of any committee report made to the membership of both House and Senate and available to the members before floor action upon the measure.

4. The position of counsel in charge of the Senate and House Office of Legislative Counsel (or other designee), and of the director of the Office of Legislative Counsel (or other designee) in the Department of Justice, should be classified at a compensation rate equal to the compensation provided for an assistant Attorney General of the United States. It is also recommended that they and the staff assistants in the three offices should be adequate in number and be assured of continuity of employment through receiving the substantive and procedural protections provided for employees in the classified civil service of the United States; and that their rates of compensation adequately reflect the skill, complexity, and judgment factors inherent in their duties and functions. This recommendation is important in several respects. If implemented it will help to attract highly qualified persons who are necessary if Congress is to effectively carry out its lawmaking function. Stability of service is significant since many of the skills involved require training beyond that usual in government service, and to assure that the judgment may be exercised and professional opinions rendered without limitation due to bureaucratic, political, partisan, or philosophical pressures within either branch of government.

An official of the administration, an independent board or commission, or a member of Congress, considering whether to support or oppose a legislative proposal, should be free to make his own decision if he disagrees with a particular staff analysis and report, but he should be able to rely upon the completely objective and professional quality of such staff reports, uninfluenced by political, social, or philosophical concerns in coming to a decision. An administrative official, independent board or commission, or member of Congress thus would be free to recommend enactment of bills that contain review reports questioning proposed provisions. Counsel's opinions would not substitute for judicial opinions or be given greater weight in any subsequent judicial review that they would be accorded in other circumstances. Their sole objective would be to guide and notify administrative officials and legislators during the course of the legislative process with respect to a constitutional problem of magnitude insofar as it may be presented in statutory proposals and to do this in such a manner as to provide a reasonable likelihood that clear statements of legislative policies will be adopted in lieu of vague and ambiguous declarations of statutory objectives.

Thus also, the administrative agency should be able to overrule its counsel's opinion that a proposed bill before the counsel for review and report violates the rule of *delegata potestas non potest delegari* (the rule that the lawmaking power, delegated by the people to Congress, cannot be redelegated by the latter to administrative agencies). An agency should *not* be able to change counsel's opinion or to cause it to be withdrawn from the report accompanying the legislative proposal for filing with Congress under threat of loss of his position. A change of opinion after professional discussion can be expected from time to time. Protection is needed, however, against undermining the independent judgment that is vital for the purposes involved by threat of employment reprisal, whether for political, philosophical, or bureaucratic reasons.

5. Staffs of standing and special committees of the two houses should be provided in adequate number to keep all members of committees fully advised in a timely fashion and to enable the staffs to devote necessary time to analysis of any pending legislation initiated by the administration that is actively considered in committee. Such staffs should receive compensation based on general uniformity of classifications and wages with those received in the executive branch for equal skills, training, judgment, and responsibility. The committee staffs play an extremely important role in the legislative process. Their numbers generally have been less in proportion that those of executive staffs, and their compensation classifications and tenure have lagged behind the patterns in executive employment. Such legislative personnel must be relied on substantially for awareness of the problems to which this study is devoted as they directly relate to the significant legislation (including both new substantive bills and proposed amendments to existing laws) of each session of Congress. Their role in assistance to the Office of Legislative Counsel or an Office of Legislative Review in Congress is comparable to the cooperative role of agency counsel with the suggested Office of Legislative Counsel of the Department of Justice. Since they are the staff of the parent congressional committee they have more experience with the subject matter than other congressional staff. They often are in a position to explain the impact of this legislation, its history, its factual applications,

and its projected effects. To perform this role they must be equipped in number, in qualification, and in adequacy of employment compensation.

6. The presence of counsel's opinion of both the Administration and Congress on this matter in the legislative file of the bill available to each member—whether as an attachment to the committee report or brought to the attention of members of the House and Senate in another manner—will assure that this important issue automatically reaches their attention, so that they may take such action as they deem appropriate. It is recommended that any member should have the right by rule to raise a point of order at any time against taking floor action upon a bill that delegates powers to an administrative agency unless the two opinions (congressional counsel's and agency counsel's) referred to are on record and the members have had a reasonable opportunity to examine and discuss them. The provision for a point of order is solely an enforcement by notice provision, binding Congress to consider any separation of powers issue presented by the bill, but making it clear that enactment of a bill that does not follow the procedure provided or does not conform to either Counsel's opinion has no legal effect upon the bill (unless a point of order is raised and denied in violation of the rules, in which case the legal effect would be similar to that of other violations of the rules).

Recapitulating, in Congress the staff work could involve the committee or subcommittee counsel, the Office of Legislative Counsel prominently, or a new office created for staff legislative review in a single house or as a joint congressional office of legislative review for the purpose under discussion. In the case of a bill that is seriously considered for adoption in one House or both Houses, the chairman of the committee having jurisdiction over the subject matter would, as far in advance of any hearing as possible, request the staff office assigned or established as the review office provided in the rule to review the bill. The review would be in the form of an opinion stating whether or not the provisions delegating authority and discretion to the Administration are sufficiently definite to establish legislative policy in accordance with the separation of powers doctrine and to prescribe definite rules of conduct to guide the Administration. The staff would advise the committee in writing.

The Legislative Counsel or new Office of Legislative Review, as the case may be, would have access to the opinions of the Department of Justice and agency counsel on the bill. He would also have access to committee counsel to discuss the subject matter involved, to the Department of Justice, and to the general counsel of the affected administrative agency on any questions he might have. If he chose to have discussions with them he would proceed to do so, these conferences taking place much as the conferences among the administrative staff had been conducted in framing the legislative proposal originally. The conferences and interchange could result in revisions of the bill that would satisfy his questions and permit him to redraft the bill, making the necessary changes to remove any questions of vagueness of discretion being granted. He would summarize the results, attaching revisions recommended in the bill, and give his opinion to the committee. If there were no questions in the first instance, and no need for revisions, his opinion would also so state. If he had questions that were not resolved, he would give a nonconcurring opinion on the bill to the committee, stating the reasons for his inability to approve the bill after review in accordance with the rule.

The committee is thereby on notice of the staff opinions, which should be incorporated in the committee report and be available in all further voting of the committee and the membership of the two Houses. Having notice, the members of the committee are in a position to decide. They are also enabled to reach a more informed consensus upon the legislation itself, which, with suggested staff revisions, now gives a more precise picture of the legislative policy established and the powers and discretion being granted. The public is entitled to no less, particularly with respect to legislation the violation of which or of regulations adopted under the legislation carries the risk of penal consequences, as is very frequently the case. The opinions themselves would be accorded no weight by the courts in the event of future litigation.

The object of the recommendations is to secure expert staff assistance with responsibility to bring the problem together with its solution, discussed in the foregoing pages, to the attention of the members of Congress before they vote. The procedure recommended, enforced by the point of order provision, should accomplish that purpose.

In the nature of things the executive branch has an interest to promote and defend. Chapter 5 shows that the main body of laws Congress enacts today has its inception in legislative proposals issuing from the Executive, regulatory commissions, and administrative agencies generally. These proposals bear a close resemblance to other bills regularly introduced in Congress. Submission by the Administration of such proposals ready for sponsorship and introduction by members of Congress may be a convenience to the legislature. Too often, however, since they are initiated by the administration, the proposals receive less scrutiny and drafting review than their significance justifies. And as a consequence serious infractions of the doctrine of nondelegability of legislative power are becoming more and more common.

The findings of Senator Ervin's Subcommittee on the Separation of Powers, discussed in Chapter 2, graphically revealed this; and Congress increasingly began to look to the remedy of the "congressional veto": inserting provisions for legislative supervision in laws delegating various kinds of authorizations requested by administrative agencies. This kind of hit-and-miss remedy proved only a pallid solution. It is now, due to a Supreme Court decision, referred to in an earlier chapter, unavailable.

A way must now be found to face the problem directly at the time when legislative proposals are first transmitted to Congress. They should then be scrutinized with reference to whether intelligible legislative policies and standards are expressed specifically enough to guide and limit administration. A procedure that appears simple and practicable for accomplishing this essential goal has been recommended in the preceding pages. It is one that, properly coordinated, should extend the time normally involved in the legislative process by only a negligible amount—minute, in fact, compared with the issues at stake. There is no way, other than direct confrontation, to prevent excessive delegation of centralized power. As Thomas Jefferson, an admirer of New England's town meetings, once said,

> If the people—ordinary citizens—could not learn to check abuses, all the more reason to fear sweeping powers in the governing "experts" who could use those powers to enslave the blundering populace.[184]

In short, Jefferson located the center of tyrannical infection in centralized power.

James Madison declared that "... the use of words is to express ideas." The most important are the words of statutory provisions regulating the freedoms of people and the conduct of government. Statutory provisions are useless if they cannot qualify under the Madison definition. This is specially true when the provisions transfer both the regulation and the conduct from Congress to administrative agencies in language lacking in concepts appropriate to guide the agencies in how their powers are to be used: the "intelligible principle" the Supreme Court has said it looks for, the "idea expression" James Madison had in mind.

As Madison further wrote in THE FEDERALIST PAPERS, there is no benefit in laws so voluminous they cannot be read or so incoherent they cannot be understood: "Law is . . . a rule of action; but how can that be a rule, which is little known, and less fixed?"[185]

A rule, by dictionary definition, is a prescribed guide for conduct or action. Hence if a law is to be executed and observed, it should prescribe guides. These guides should be provided in the words meeting Madison's simple test that they express ideas. Only Congress can prescribe them; the Founders refused to permit delegation of the power.

A law per se requires the provision of policies and rules of conduct, enacted by the legislature by appropriate process, to be enforced and obeyed. Congress should reject uncertain and unfixed rules of action offered by the Executive and reassume its basic function. The Founders meant Congress to be the paramount branch, for reasons appearing in Chapter 3. The national legislature, however, loses by attrition a portion of its ascendant status as it delegates power of a legislative nature. The long-term effect upon the government, the people governed, and the states has been and will be unfortunate. The results will be those sought to be avoided—certainly not those intended to be a legacy—by those who labored, fought, and used all their powers of persuasion that a new land might be, and remain, free.

To "make the rules of law," as Alexander Hamilton defined the legislative function to be, is possible only with qualified staff assistance and with understanding of what is expected. The positive, simple formula recommended in this chapter and supported by the American Bar Association, as indicated by the resolution attached as Appendix I, is offered as an *aid* to that understanding. If constructively and intelligently employed, the formula should go a long way toward restoring life to and obtaining compliance with the doctrine of separation of powers.

NOTES

CHAPTER 1

1. 15 U.S.C. § 45.
2. 42 U.S.C. §§ 7401 et seq., 7601, 7602(a).
3. 42 U.S.C. § 1463 et seq.
4. 41 U.S.C. § 10 a, d.

CHAPTER 2

5. 47 U.S.C. § 151 et seq.
6. 47 U.S.C. § 315(a)(3), (4).
7. 47 U.S.C. § 151 et seq.
8. 47 U.S.C. § 731 (1962).
9. 47 U.S.C. §§ 735, 741.
10. Id. § 201; 47 C.F.R. 21.0 et seq. The FCC's regulatory authority does not preclude a telecommunication carrier from being subject to the Sherman Anti-Trust Act, Section 1-7 of Title 15, U.S. Code, with respect to actions not expressly exempt by law, *MCI Communications Corp. v. American Tel. & Tel. Co.*, 708 F.2d 1081 (7th Cir. 1983), *cert. denied,* _____ U.S. (1983—no U.S. citation yet available), 104 S. Ct. 234; *Mid-Texas Communications Systems, Inc. v. American Tel. & Tel. Co.*, 615 F. 2d 1372 (5th Cir. 1980), *cert. denied sub nom. Woodlands Telecommunications Corp. v. Southwestern Bell Tel. Co.*, 449 U.S. 912, 101 S. Ct. 286, 66 L. Ed. 2d 140.
11. 47 U.S.C. § 307(c) (as amended in 1981 and 1982).
12. Id. § 308(b).
13. Id. § 307(a).
14. Id. § 307(b).
15. Id. § 303(f).
16. Id. § 326.

---

*Because the sources cited throughout the book are drawn chiefly from legal authorities, they are cited in accordance with the style set out in A UNIFORM SYSTEM OF CITATION (Cambridge, Mass.: Harvard Law Review Association, 13th Ed., 1981), which is authoritative in the legal profession. Further, it is anticipated that readers pursuing further study will be directed to law libraries and are better served by legal citation.

However, Chapter 3 (Constitutional History) draws also upon sources normally accessible outside the legal profession. Thus, the citations in that chapter are made in accordance with generally accepted journalistic custom.

17. *National Broadcasting Co. v. United States,* 319 U.S. 190, 87 L. Ed. 1344 (1942).

18. 47 U.S.C. § 309(a).

19. *Universal Camera Corp. v. NLRB,* 340 U.S. 474, 71 S. Ct. 456, 95 L. Ed. 456 (1951).

20. *National Cable Television Ass'n. v. United States,* 415 U.S. 336, 94 S. Ct. 1146, 39 L. Ed. 2d 370 (1974).

21. *Columbia Broadcasting Companies v. Democratic National Committee,* 412 U.S. 94, 93 S. Ct. 2080, 36 L. Ed. 2d 772 (1973).

22. John A. Carver, *Administrative Law and Public Land Management,* 18 ADMIN. L. REV. 7, 11 (1965).

23. Donald E. Schwinn, *Public Land Law Review Commission Report—Oracle or Ogre?* 4 NATURAL RESOURCES LAWYER 168, 171 (1971).

24. Carver, *Administrtive Law and Public Land Management 12.*

25. *One Third of the Nation's Land,* a Report to the President and to the Congress by the Public Land Law Review Commission, June 20, 1970 (Hereinafter referred to as Report of the Commission).

26. 30 U.S.C. § 22 (1964).

27. Id., § 23.

28. Extract from letter to the author from Frederic L. Kirgis.

29. Statement of Frederic L. Kirgis to the Public Land Law Review Commission, Hearings, March 25, 1966.

30. Report of the Commission 130.

31. 33 U.S.C. § 1251 et seq.

32. The National Labor Relations Act, as amended, 29 U.S.C. § 141 et seq.

33. Part 1, *Hearings on Separation of Powers,* NLRB Hearings before the Subcommittee on Separation of Powers of the Senate Committee on the Judiciary, 90th Cong., 1st Sess. (1967) (hereinafter referred to as Separation of Powers Hearings), p. 1:

> The goal of the Subcommittee on Separation of Powers is: To make a full and complete study of the separation of powers between the executive, judiciary, and legislative branches of government provided by the Constitution, the manner in which power has been exercised by each branch, and the extent, if any, to which any branch or branches of the government may have encroached upon the powers, functions, and duties vested in any other branch by the Constitution of the United States.

34. Senator Sam J. Ervin, Jr. (D., N.C.), *Separation of Powers,* XXXV Vital Speeches of the Day (November 5, 1969), 189, 192.

35. Report of the Senate Committee on the Judiciary, Subcommittee on Separation of Powers, Congressional Oversight of Administrative Agencies

(NLRB), 91st Cong., 1st Sess. (1970), p. 19 (hereinafter referred to as the Committee Report).

36. Id. p. 5.

37. 149 N.L.R.B. 67 (1964).

38. *Allis-Chalmers Mfg. Co. v. NLRB*, 358 F.2d 656 (7 Cir. 1966).

39. *NLRB v. Allis-Chalmers Mfg. Co.*, 388 U.S. 175, 87 S. Ct. 2001, 18 L. Ed. 2d 1123 (1967).

40. Separation of Powers Hearings, 1669-70.

41. *NLRB v. Gissel Packing Co.*, 395 U.S. 575, 89 S. Ct. 1918, 23 L. Ed. 2d 547 (1969).

42. *Linden Lumber Division, Summer & Co. v. NLRB*, 419 U.S. 301, 95 S. Ct. 429, 42 L. Ed. 2d 465 (1974) (four justices dissenting).

43. P.L. 89-174, 89th Cong., 79 Stat. 667, 5 U.S.C. § 624, September 9, 1965.

44. P.L. 81-171, 63 Stat. 413, 42 U.S.C. 1441.

45. 42 U.S.C. § 1450 et seq. For an excellent discussion, see H.N. Osgood & A.H. Zwerner, *Rehabilitation and Conservation*, 25 LAW & CONTEMP. PROBS. 705 (1960).

46. 42 U.S.C. § 1460 (c), as amended in 1964.

47. P.L. 89-754 (1966); 42 U.S.C. § 3301 et seq. (omitted pursuant to 42 U.S.C. § 5316, which terminated authority to make grants and loans after January 1, 1975).

48. Hearings before the Subcommittee on Housing, Committee on Banking and Currency, House of Representatives, 87th Cong., 1st Sess. on H.R. 6028, H.R. 5300, and H.R. 6423 (April 24 to May 5, 1961), p. 93:

Mr. Widnall. Would I, as a Congressman making $22,500 a year, be eligible to buy one of these loans with a 40-year loan and no downpayment?

Mr. Weaver. Theoretically, yes. In some cases, of course, preference in the sale will be given to displaced families.

49. 42 U.S.C. § 1453 (1978).

50. P.L. 88-408, 78 Stat. 384.

51. U.S. Department of Defense, UNITED STATES VIETNAM RELATIONS 1945-1967, Vol. 12, Part. VI.B., p. 3.

52. KEETING'S TREATIES AND ALLIANCES OF THE WORLD (Bristol, England, 1968), pp. 187-89.

53. 1964 U.S. CODE CONG. AND ADMIN. NEWS (88th Cong., 2d Sess.), 2685.

54. Senate Foreign Relations Committee, *U.S. Commitments to Foreign Powers*, Hearings on Senate Resolution 151, August and September 1967, p. 82; see also p. 83. In a State Department Position Paper, the historical argument *building* upon the constitutional power of the President as commander-in-chief was illustrated:

Since the Constitution was adopted, there have been at least 125 instances in which the President, without Congressional authority and in the absence of a declaration of war, has ordered the Armed Forces to take actions or to maintain positions abroad. Some of these historical instances have involved the use of U.S. forces in combat. (State Department Position Paper, THE QUESTION OF A FORMAL DECLARATION OF WAR IN VIETNAM, November 19, 1965, p. 2.)

There was evidence in the 1967 hearings, however, indicating that the incidents cited were clearly minor actions and justifiable either on the grounds of protection of American lives and property or as military acts of pure self-defense in which the demand for action was immediate. (Statement of Nicholas Katzenbach, *Commitments to Foreign Powers* 81; and see F. Wurmuth, THE VIETNAM WAR: THE PRESIDENT VERSUS THE CONSTITUTION 35 (1968), for factual analysis.) Also, "[s]ome of the instances grouped within the 125 presidential uses of force are erroneously included, chiefly the Naval War with France of 1798–1800 and the Barbary Wars of 1801–05 and 1815, which were conducted with specific congressional approval." (W. Reveley, *Presidential War-Making, Constitutional Prerogative or Usurpation*, 55 VA. L. REV. 1243, 1290 [1969]). But there was also evidence that could not be lightly dismissed. Secretary of Defense Robert McNamara noted that ". . . [t]he Formosa resolution of 1955 was followed by the use of U.S. warships to escort supply convoys to the offshore islands in 1958; the Cuba resolution was followed by the well-known events of October 1962. . . ." 1964 U.S. CODE CONG. AND ADMIN. NEWS, 2676, 2685, 88th Cong., 2d Sess.

55. Separation of Powers Hearings, July, August, September 1967, p. 47. Mr. Justice Robert Jackson made it clear as a matter of constitutional doctrine, in *Youngstown Sheet & Tube Co. v. Sawyer*, 343 U.S. 579, 642, 73 S. Ct. 863, 873 (1952) (concurring opinion), that no principle was stronger than that of vesting the war power in the body most representative of the people: ". . . Nothing in our Constitution is plainer than that declaration of a war is entrusted only to Congress. . . ." In Mr. Justice Black's words, ". . . [t]he Founders of this Nation entrusted the law-making power to the Congress alone in both good and bad times. . . ." (Id. 587, 589).

56. As cited in Separation of Powers Hearings, p. 182.

57. The form that congressional authority should take is one of policy, committed to the discretion of Congress, and outside the power and competence of the judiciary because there are no intelligible and objectively manageable standards by which to judge such actions (citing *Baker v. Carr* 369 U.S. 186, 82 S. Ct. 691, 7 L. Ed. 2d 663 [1962]). See, *Berk v. Laird*, 317 F. Supp. 715 (E.D.N.Y. 1970), *aff'd*, 443 F. 2d 1039 (2d Cir. 1971), *cert. denied*, 404 U.S. 869, 92 S. Ct. 94, 30 L. Ed. 2d 113. Circuit Judge Irving R. Kaufman concurred on the basis of adoption by Congress of the Tonkin Gulf Resolution and clear evidence of continuing and distinctly expressed participation by the legislative branch in the prosecution of

the war. (The Senate repealed the Tonkin Gulf Resolution on June 24, 1970 [Cong. Record S. 9670, June 24, 1970; see Foreign Military Sales Act of 1971 § 12, P.L. 91–672, January 12, 1971]), see also *Massachusetts v. Laird,* 451 F.2d 26 (1st Cir. 1971); *Meyers v. Nixon,* 339 F. Supp. 1388 (S.D.N.Y. 1972).

CHAPTER 3

58. The hypothetical statute and question are paraphrased with one exception from Chief Judge (U.S. Court of Appeals, 2d Circuit) Henry J. Friendly's question in *Benchmarks* (Chicago: University of Chicago Press 1967), p. 103; see also his article, *The Federal Administrative Agencies: The Need for Better Definition of Standards,* 75 HARV. L. REV. 863, 880 (note 84), 1055, 1263, (1962). The exception is this. Judge Friendly would apparently consider the statute more favorably if the agency "after proper investigation supplies the principles that Congress didn't and perhaps couldn't furnish. . . ." He observes, with respect to the hypothetical statutory command in the text, that, even if the statute were deemed to comply with the literal requirement of the Constitution that all legislative powers granted shall be vested in Congress, "and we do not believe it does—it hardly complies with the spirit." (75 HARV. L. REV. 863, 872, 880.) Sometimes telling the agency to do what is in the public interest, in Judge Friendly's opinion, is the "practical equivalent" of the hypothetical injunction set forth in the text.

59. There was no provision for a chief executive. Congress was authorized to appoint "a Committee of the States" Congress of the United States, consisting of one delegate from each state, to sit in the recesses of Congress and execute powers delegated to them by Congress. Congress was also authorized to appoint other committees and civil officers to manage the general affairs of the United States, but under the direction of Congress. (Articles of Confederation, Article 9.)

The Articles of Confederation failed to provide a central government of adequate strength for the new nation. The Articles, it has been said, granted powers to the Congress "which it had already been exercising, and significantly they were essentially those of Parliament and the Crown under the old empire." A. Kelly & W. Harbison, *The American Constitution: Its Origin and Development* (New York: W. W. Norton & Co., 1963), p.101. The Articles were a legal codification of the powers of the extralegal Continental Congresses that had been operating the nation's affairs since May 1775.

The Articles were not ratified until March 1781. James Madison, Jr., of Virginia, in his *Journal of the Federal Convention,* (Chicago: Albert, Scott & Co., ed. E.H. Scott, 1893), p. 31, says that the difficulties experienced during the five-year ratification struggle may be traced to—first, the natural repugnance of the parties to a relinquishment of power; secondly, a natural jealousy of its abuse in other hands than their own; thirdly, the rules of suffrage among parties whose inequality in size did not correspond to their wealth, their military or free population; fourthly, the selection and definition of the powers, at once necessary to the federal head, and safe to the several members. ("Introduction," pp. 32–33.)

Additionally, Madison cites as a difficulty the disposal of Crown lands and the fact that "some of the States ... having no convenient ports for foreign commerce were subject to be taxed by their neighbors, through whose ports their commerce was carried on." (JOURNAL, "Introduction," p. 33. (Subsequent references will be to the JOURNAL itself and will be made by date only).

The analysis of the Articles of Confederation is based on the text of the articles printed in *Documents of American History*, (New York: Appleton-Century-Crofts, Commanger ed. 1962), 111–115. The Congress established under the Articles of Confederation was given exclusive power to make war and peace, to negotiate treaties and alliances, to send and receive ambassadors, to try cases of piracy and felony committed on the high seas, to fix standards of weights and measures, to regulate Indian affairs, and to establish and operate a nationwide postal system. On matters of importance, specified in the articles, the vote of two-thirds of the states was required to authorize Congress to act. Among the specific areas mentioned were declaration of war, confirmation of treaties, regulation of the value of coinage, borrowing and appropriating money, and building land and naval forces.

Two of the most important powers of a national government were denied to the Congress under the Articles of Confederation: the power to tax, and the power to regulate commerce.

Based proportionately on the assessed value of property of each state, sums of money could be requested by the Confederation Congress from the states to be used as a national treasury for the common defense and general welfare. In addition, the Congress could train and maintain an army and navy, requesting both needed men and money from each state in accordance with the same apportioning principle. The states stipulated that while the Congress had the power to negotiate treaties and alliances, nonetheless it was not authorized to sign a treaty that would infringe upon the states' right to retaliate against foreign commercial discrimination effected against any of the states. Full faith and credit were to be quaranteed to the laws of each state. Citizens of any state were to be afforded the privileges and immunities granted the citizens of any other state. In disputes between the states, Congress was to be the final arbiter. Congress was authorized by the articles to administer the national affairs through establishment of congressional committees that, during congressional recesses, could act in specified instances in the name of "congress assembled." The discontent with the articles can be traced to one basic deficiency inherent in the system: the inability of the Congress to enforce compliance with any law it passed. The deficiency was manifest in two areas of legislation: the power to collect taxes, and the power to regulate commerce. Specifically, Congress was unable to establish a sound fiscal policy and issue sound currency; it was repeatedly embarrassed by its inability to meet the interest on outstanding debts, not to mention the debts themselves. It had no power forcibly to draft men or collect money within the states, and as a consequence, it could not adequately provide for the common defense. Its inability to force the states to comply with the terms of the Treaty of Paris (1783) convinced foreign powers that the United States was a poor financial risk and a fertile field for imperialistic expansion.

Many of these defects are detailed in the debates of the Constitutional Convention (1787) and in the various FEDERALIST PAPERS.As reported in James Madison's distinctive style, for example, on May 29, 1787, in the Constitutional Convention, Edmund Randolph (Virginia) listed the defects within the Articles, saying

> First, that the Confederation produced no security against foreign invasion; Congress not being permitted to prevent a war, nor to support it by their own authority. Of this [Randolph] cited many examples; most of which tended to show, that they could not cause infractions of treaties, or of the law of nations to be punished; that particular States might by their conduct provoke war without control; and that, neither militia nor drafts being fit for defense on such occasions, enlistments only could be successful, and these could not be executed without money.

> Secondly, that the Federal Government could not check the quarrel between the States, nor a rebellion in any, not having constitutional power nor means to impose according to the exigency.

> Thirdly, that there were many advantages which the United States might acquire, which were not attainable under the Confederation—such as a productive impost—counteraction of the commercial regulations of other nations—pushing of commerce *ad libitum,* & c., & c.

> Fourthly, that the Federal Government could not defend itself against encroachments from the States.

> Fifthly, that it was not even paramount to the State Constitutions, ratified as it was in many of the States. (Madison,JOURNAL,May 29.)

60. There had been earlier attempts at union, prior to the Articles of Confederation, but they were far more informal and restrictive in conception, and their relevancy to this study is remote. The founding of the New England Confederation (1643–1684), the first successful coalescence, was a qualified association of four colonies: Massachusetts, Connecticut, Plymouth, and New Haven. Between 1643 and 1788, when the Philadelphia Constitution was ratified, many forms of union among the thirteen colonies were attempted. W. H. Bennett, *American Theories of Federalism* (Ala.: University of Alabama Press, 1964), p. 37. A second attempt at intercolonial confederation was proposed in 1697 by William Penn. The Daniel Cox plan in 1726 provided for economic cooperation and mutual defense among the members. The Albany Plan was prompted in 1754 by the impending French and Indian War, and suggested by Benjamin Franklin. J. D. Hicks, *The Federal Union* (Boston: Houghton Mifflin Co., 1952), p. 99. The fifth plan was presented by Joseph Galloway to the First Continental Congress in 1744; the Second Continental Congress convened in 1775. Kelly and Harbison, THE AMERICAN CONSTITUTION, p. 93. With the failure of the conciliatory approach, Congress authorized a delegation to draft the Declaration of Independence in June 1776, and it was adopted by the Congress on July 4, 1776. A committee also was appointed "to prepare a 'form of confederation.' " Max Farrand, *The Framing of the Constitution of the United States* (New Haven, Conn.: Yale University Press (1913), p. 2.

The colonies (by now called states) were reluctant to ratify the resulting document, the Articles of the Confederation; and the Articles were not officially operative until Maryland ratified them in March 1781. In the interim period, the Continental Congress acted as a central committee to conduct the war and foreign relations. Kelly and Harbison note that the far-sighted Congress

> very early encouraged the formation of regularized state governments. In June 1775 it suggested to the Massachusetts provisional congress that it would be wise to erect a new government which would restore to the Commonwealth the privileges of the original charter, and in November it made a like recommendation to New Hampshire and South Carolina. . . . In May 1776, the Congress ordered the formal suppression of all remnants of royal authority in the states so that the way was then cleared for the erection of permanent constitutional systems. Between 1776 and 1780, therefore, all the states except two adopted new written constitutions. In Rhode Island and Connecticut the old charters were still regarded as acceptable forms of government, and they continued to serve well into the nineteenth century. (THE AMERICAN CONSTITUTION, p. 94.)

The state constitutions, therefore, were antecedent to any national plan of union later adopted. The only central authority that the states would accept was a general legislature; and, in restricted cases during recesses, the powers of the legislature were implemented by an appointed committee acting in the name of the "congress assembled." *Documents of American History,* p. 114.

Article II of the Articles of Confederation clearly defines the status of the states: "Each state retains its sovereignty, freedom and independence, and every Power, Jurisdiction and right, which is not by this confederation expressly delegated to the United States, in Congress assembled."

61. The suggestion to use the word "Philadelphia" to describe the Constitution written in 1787, as I will use it here, is offered by Professors Willmore Kendall and George W. Carey (in their introduction to the Heirloom Edition of THE FEDERALIST PAPERS, New York: Arlington House, 1965, as a reference to the Constitution without the Bill of Rights, which Hamilton, Madison, and Jay were explaining and defending in THE FEDERALIST PAPERS under the pseudonym "Publius."

62. The Philadelphia Constitution was written to implement specific republican principles that were considered to be essential to the desired guarantee of individual liberty. The debates in the Constitutional Convention and the arguments in the FEDERALIST clearly show the concern of the Founding Fathers for "common defense, security of liberty, and general welfare." (Madison, JOURNAL,May 29)

In addition, as Professor James Burnham says, "the ideas of 'division of power,' [and] 'check and balance' are at the irradicable core of the American governmental tradition." *Congress and the American Tradition* (Chicago: Henry Regnery Co., 1965) p. 37. These were the basic means of securing a badly needed, strong central government for the people. Equally, they provided the citizens of the United States with the maximum of personal liberty. These principles, too, are borne out by the debates in the Philadelphia Convention that will now be considered.

According to the greatest political thinkers of the time, among them Madison, Hamilton, and Jay, the problems of the Union were not to be satisfied by a stronger *Confederation.*

The Virginia Plan brought the problem of a change in general government to the attention of the delegates. Its adoption, as symbolized by the exclusive consideration by the Convention of the nineteen resolutions, marked the demise of the Articles of Confederation. The delegates voted to take upon themselves the responsibility of creating a new form of union—with or without the specific authorization of their respective states—and when the new form was drafted and finally adopted by the Convention, it should be submitted to the people of the several United States for ratification, thereby circumventing the state legislatures, which thus would have no part in authorizing it. The Founding Fathers considered the state legislatures to be too democratically controlled, for example, too prone to tax and too unsympathetic to property rights and capital. F. Rodell, *Fifty-Five Men* (Harrisburg, Pa.: Telegraph Press, 1936), p.20.

63. The Virginia Plan, which was placed before the delegates at Philadelphia, did not attempt to eliminate state participation completely in the central government. However, this fact was not apparent to many of the delegates—particularly the delegates from the small states and their spokesman, William Paterson of New Jersey. To some extent the resolution of this problem came in the decision to leave the appointment of Senate members to the state legislatures, which presumably demonstrated state control over half of the national legislature. The national lawmaking body, also, was denied the authority to negate state laws on the basis that this would mark the political disintegration of the small states. It should be noted in this connection that Luther Martin, of Maryland, successfully proposed a resolution, which became Article VI of the Philadelphia Constitution, that the Articles of the Union (the Constitution) would be the supreme law of the land and that the judiciaries of the states would be bound by them, "anything in the respective laws of the individual state to the contrary notwithstanding." (Madison, JOURNAL, July 17) This assured the supremacy of the U.S. government over the states in the federal field.

A concise summary of the spheres of operation of both the states and the central government was given by Hamilton soon after the Convention. His definition of the limits of the central government in particular was:

> An entire consolidation of the States into one complete national sovereignty would imply an entire subordination of the parts; and whatever powers might remain in them would be altogether dependent on the general will. But as the plan of the convention aims only at a partial union or consolidation, the State governments would clearly retain all the rights of sovereignty which they before had, and which were not, by that act [of ratification] *exclusively* delegated to the United States. This exclusive delegation, or rather this alienation, of State Sovereignty would only exist in three cases: where the Constitution in express terms granted an exclusive authority to the Union; where it granted in one instance an authority to the Union, and in another prohibited the States from exercising the like authority; and where it granted an authority to the Union to which a similar authority in the States would be absolutely and totally contradictory. . . . (FEDERALIST, No. 32)

64. Rodell, *Fifty-Five Men*, p. 20; C. Beard, *An Economic Interpretation of the Constitution of the United States* (New York: Free Press, 1965), p. 221.

65. FEDERALIST, No. 51. See also Alexander Hamilton's declaration of intention of the founders in FEDERALIST, No. 32, and Charles Pinckney's emphasis on preserving local rights mentioned in Madison, JOURNAL, June 25.

66. A. Vanderbilt, *The Doctrine of the Separation of Powers and Its Present-Day Significance*, (Lincoln, Neb.: University of Nebraska Press, 1953), p. 48. Vanderbilt was Chief Justice of the Supreme Court of New Jersey.

Hamilton and Madison said on many occasions in *The Federalist* that the national government would operate on individuals and not on the states as collective entities so that the central government could be one of laws and not one of force. Specifically, Hamilton says that

> [t]he majesty of the national authority must be manifested through the medium of the courts of justice. The government of the Union, like that of each State, must be able to address itself immediately to the hopes and fears of individuals; and to attract to its support those passions which have the strongest influence upon the human heart. (FEDERALIST, No. 16.)

Hamilton continues that it is logical to think that either a direct negative on state laws must be given the national legislature or there "must be an authority in the federal courts to overrule such as might be in manifest contravention of the articles of union."(FEDERALIST,No. 80.) This passage brings out clearly the recognition of the possibility of future conflict over the extent of both central and state authority and powers and the need to provide a means to solve the conflict in a way upholding appropriate exercise of power by the central government. According to the working of the Constitution, the *state* courts were bound to hold the Constitution as the supreme law of the land. The only possible purpose, therefore, for instituting a national supreme judiciary would be to interpret constitutional powers and duties and the laws implementing the Constitution as well as to enable the executive to execute faithfully those laws.

67. Charles Louis de Secondat, Baron de Brede et de Montesquieu, *The Spirit of the Laws XI* (New York: Hafner Publishing Co. 1949).

68. John Foster Hall Sherwood, *The Theory of the Separation of Powers in Its Relation to Administrative Legislation and Adjudication* (Ph.D. diss., University of California, Los Angeles, 1941), pp. 19–20.

69. FEDERALIST Nos. 47–51. It is sometimes said that Montesquieu completely misconstrued the British system as practicing strict separation of powers. He did; but the misconstruction had little to do with his advocacy of separation of powers. Moreover, his incorrect impression of the British practice may well have been due to a visit made by the Baron, toward the end of a lengthy sojourn in Britain, to Parliament, when he is said to have observed that administrative officials were not allowed on the floor of the Houses of Parliament, a temporary Parliamentary restraint that was removed shortly after his return to France. Struck by what he had seen, he considered this a perfect illustration of separation of powers. The restraint never prevailed beyond this in Britain, however, though it does in the United States. In George Washington's day, when as President he sought to sit down with Congress on a thorny legislative issue, his request was haughtily denied on the ground of separation of powers. Today government officials are not generally allowed in the floors of Congress when that body is in session.

70. See Chapter 4.

71. Montesquieu, *The Spirit of the Laws,* pp. 150–52.

72. Article I, Section 1: "All legislative powers herein granted shall be vested in a Congress of the United States...." Article II, Section 1: "The executive power shall be vested in a President...." Article III, Section 1: "The judicial power of the United States, shall be vested in one supreme Court, and in such inferior Courts as the Congress may from time to time ordain and establish...."

73. *Federalist,* No. 51.

74. Madison's solution to the predictable situation of overlapping powers, which the Philadelphia Constitution reflects, was to establish an interacting structure of government so contrived "that its several constituent parts may, by their mutual relations, be the means of keeping each other in their proper places." (FEDERALIST, No. 51.) That is, "opposite and rival interests" are stated, divided, and arranged "in such a manner so that each may be a check on the other—that the private interest of every individual may be a sentinel over the public rights." (FEDERALIST, No. 51.) Although in the Convention he was arguing, somewhat inconsistently, for a Council of Revision, composed of the judiciary and the executive, which would decide the constitutionality of laws passed by the legislature, Madison voiced the basic idea of construction, which was agreed to in general by the delegates. He urged:

> If a constitutional discrimination of the departments on paper were a sufficient security to each against encroachments of the others, all further provisions would indeed be superfluous. But experience had taught us a distrust of that security.... (JOURNAL, June 21.)

The matter of composing the legislature and delegating to it powers and defenses was one of the most complex and knotty problems of the convention. As a legislature was the form of government existing at the time, it was the most familiar to the delegates. And as the existing legislature, under the Articles of Confederation, represented the states as states, the natural inclination of most of the delegates was to incorporate this kind of a legislature in the new form of union. Moreover, the idea of state sovereignty spoke of state equality to many members, and they consequently insisted that each state be given equal voice in the national legislature. The proponents of the new central government, on the other hand, insisted that the government would operate directly on the citizens as individuals and that, therefore, representation in the national legislature should reflect population.

On July 16 a set of compromise resolutions was passed that stated that there would be an equality of votes in the Senate, that a proportional representation of state inhabitants would make up the House, and that money appropriation bills and salaries of officers of the United States would originate in the House of Representatives, not to be amended by the Senate. (Madison, JOURNAL, July 16.)

By means of this compromise—or, in other terms, by means of the composition of both Houses of Congress—a balance would be effected between the large and small states, which would have an equal voice in the Senate and the members of which the state legislatures would appoint, plus a balance between the states in the Senate and the "headstrong citizenry" in the House. The Senate and House had mutual protection against either gaining ascendancy over the legislature and, in the last resort, the nation, by means of a mutual veto of proposed laws. As a further check on the influence of the national legislature, no member of the Senate or House could hold another public office while serving in the national legislature. Finally, the House could not vote increases in its salaries or those of the members of the Senate to take effect during their term of office.

75. FEDERALIST, No. 78.

76. Professor Morris D. Forkosch, in his text on CONSTITUTIONAL LAW (Mineola, NY: Foundation Press, 1963), pp. 12–13, discusses a Supreme Court opinion by Chief Justice William Taft in 1923 that illustrates this. The court upheld a Presidential pardon of an individual who had been found guilty of criminal contempt of court, rejecting the view of the lower federal court that the President's action threatened the independence of the judiciary and thus violated the doctrine of separation of powers. Complete independence and separation among the three branches were not intended, the court declared, though a qualified independence, each of the other, was provided. Thus the opinion cited the provision giving life tenure to judges, an independence balanced in part by the congressional power to impeach judges; the provision for faithful execution of the laws and executive pardons, balanced by congressional power over appropriations and confirmation of executive appointees; and the provision for executive veto of any legislation. Chief Justice Taft observed: "The fact is that the Judiciary, quite as much as Congress and the Executive, are dependent on the cooperation of the other two, that government may go on."

77. Specific powers granted to Congress included the power to enact appropriations (Article I, Section 7); to lay and collect taxes (Article I, Section 8, Clause 1), duties, imposts, and excises, to pay the debts and provide for the common defense and general welfare of the United States; to declare war (Article I, Section 8), to grant letters of marque and reprisal and to make rules concerning captures on land and water; to regulate commerce (Article I, Section 8) with foreign nations, and among the several states, and with the Indian tribes; to define and punish piracies and felonies committed on the high seas and offences against the Law of Nations (Article I, Section 8); and to make all laws necessary and proper for carrying into effect the foregoing powers, and all other powers vested by the Constitution in the U.S. government. The powers referred to are not a complete recitation of congressional powers as conferred, and some of those unmentioned, such as the power to coin money, establish a uniform rule of naturalization, enact uniform rules on the subject of bankruptcies, and grant copyrights and patents, although important, were not considered at any length in the Convention.

78. Madison, JOURNAL, August 17.

79. FEDERALIST, No. 29. Hamilton continues in the same framework in FEDERALIST, No. 33. Essentially, the "necessary and proper" clause in combination with the "supreme law of the land" clause

> [is] only declaratory of a truth which would have resulted by necessary and unavoidable implication from the very act of constituting a federal government and vesting it with certain specified powers.

He comments that the members of the Convention inserted the clause because they

> probably foresaw ... that the danger which most threatens our political welfare is that the State government will finally sap the foundations of the Union; and might therefore think it necessary, in so cardinal a point, to leave nothing to construction. (FEDERALIST, No. 33.)

80. FEDERALIST, No. 33.

81. FEDERALIST, No. 44.

82. FEDERALIST, No. 45.

83. Hamilton said that the treaty-making power of its very nature is mixed. It is legislative in the sense that its provisions have the force of law, but it is also executive in that treaties are "agreements between sovereign and sovereign." FEDERALIST, No. 75.

84. FEDERALIST, Nos. 69, 70.

85. M. Farrand, *The Records of the Federal Convention of 1787.* Vol. 1 (New Haven, Conn: Yale University Press, Rev. Ed., 1937, at pages 62-67, hereinafter referred to as RECORDS.) Also Madison, JOURNAL, June 1: At the outset, the large issues in the debate centered primarily around the extent of the powers of the proposed executive with a view to determining whether or not a single or plural executive would be more proper to hold the executive power safely.

In Sherman's view,

> the executive magistracy [was] nothing more than an institution for carrying the will of the legislature into effect; ... the person or persons ought to be appointed by and accountable to the legislature only, which was the depository of the supreme will of the society. As they were the best judges of the business which ought to be done by the executive department, and consequently of the number necessary from time to time for doing it, he wished the number might not be fixed, but that the legislature should be at liberty to appoint one or more as experience might dictate.

Wilson stated that it was his belief that the powers of the executive should not include any of a legislative nature, and he gave as an example the power of making war and peace:

> the only powers he considered strictly executive were those of executing the law, and appointing officers, not appertaining to, and appointed by, the legislature. (Madison, JOURNAL, June 1.)

86. Madison, JOURNAL, June 1.

87. Madison, JOURNAL, June 1.

88. Farrand, RECORDS, p. 67, Madison, JOURNAL, June 1. Madison's motion is quoted in the text, the delegation clause that caused controversy being underlined for emphasis. After Committee action on Pinckney's first objection to the delegation clause in Madison's motion, the delegation clause of the motion now read: "and to execute such other powers not legislative nor judiciary in their nature as may from time to time be delegated by the national legislature." When Pinckney described the delegation clause, amended at his suggestion as "unnecessary," his clear meaning was that the clause added nothing to the first part of the same motion giving the President power to carry out the national laws. If its effect were greater, Committee members expressed views that they would be opposed for this reason. And thus Pinckney's description of the stricken words as "unnecessary, their object being included in the power to carry into effect the national laws [see above] . . ." must be considered in the context in which it was given. The "unnecessary" remark was directed to the above-quoted portion of the Madison resolution amended by Pinckney's motion. If it had been directed to the Madison motion as originally stated (authorizing the President to execute such other powers as from time to time may be delegated) an argument could be made that calling the stricken authorization unnecessary as already included in the power to carry into effect the national laws is evidence that the existing authorization would permit Congress to delegate any power it wished. That argument is not available. Pinckney's amendment to that motion, accepted by all delegates voting, already had restricted the motion's scope. It was the amended Madison resolution with this restriction incorporated in it that Pinckney viewed as repetitious of the executive's constitutional authority to carry out the national laws provided for in the Madison motion. As has been noted, Madison agreed with Pinckney's view but felt it did no harm to add the clause. A majority of the Committee supported General Pinckney however. The retained portion of Madison's motion with the delegation clause omitted, was as follows: "*that a national Executive ought to be instituted with power to carry into effect the national laws and to appoint to offices in cases not otherwise provided for. . .*"

89. Madison, JOURNAL, May 31.

90. Farrand, RECORDS, p. 67.

91. Madison, JOURNAL, June 1.

92. FEDERALIST, No. 70.

93. FEDERALIST, No. 69.

94. FEDERALIST, No. 69.

95. FEDERALIST, No. 70.

96. Madison, JOURNAL, June 1.

97. Madison, JOURNAL, August 24.

98. Madison, JOURNAL, August 24.

99. Madison, JOURNAL, August 24.

100. Madison, JOURNAL, August 24.

101. Madison, JOURNAL, September 7.

102. Madison, JOURNAL, September 7. The first case dealing with the President's power of removal of an executive appointee--a contingency not expressly provided for in the Constitution--involved a law that provided for a four-year appointment term for postmasters. President Woodrow Wilson asked for the resignation of a postmaster and when it was not forthcoming, summarily removed him. The dismissal occurred before the end of the four-year term, and the President made no charges against the postmaster, gave him no hearing, and did not consult the Senate. The court held in the case of *Myers v. United States* 272 U.S. 52, 47 S. Ct. 21, 71 L. Ed. 160 (1926), that the dismissal was valid, Chief Justice Taft writing for the Court, with Justices Holmes, McReynolds and Brandeis dissenting. The Court ruled that the executive power is vested in the President, that to carry out this power and the power to see that the laws are faithfully executed, he must of necessity act through subordinates. To obtain responsible assistance, the Court said that the removal power was indispensable and could not be limited by the Congress. In reaching this conclusion the Court said that the power to appoint conveys by implication the power to remove and that the President received this power as a matter of constitutional grant, which took precedence over any statute. The Court also stressed the founders' intention to separate legislative from executive functions due to their firm belief in Baron de Montesquieu's views. The Chief Justice stressed that one of the chief purposes of the Convention, according to Madison, was to separate the legislative from the executive functions, since their union under the confederation "had not worked well, as the members of the Convention knew. Montesquieu's view that the maintenance of independence as between the legislative, the executive and the judicial branches was a security for the people had their full approval. . . . From this division on principle, the reasonable construction of the Constitution must be that the branches should be kept separate in all cases in which they were not expressly blended, and the Constitution should be expounded to blend them no more than it affirmatively requires. Madison, 1 ANNALS OF CONGRESS, 497. This rule of construction has been confirmed by this Court. . . ." (71 L. Ed. at 166.)

President Franklin D. Roosevelt, in 1933, dismissed a member off the Federal Trade Commission who had been appointed to a fixed term in office by

President Herbert Hoover under a statute fixing the office as having a five-year term. The statute provided for removal from office only for "inefficiency, neglect of duty or malfeasance in office." The President made no such charge, notifying the commissioner only that he did not feel that their minds "go along together." His duties under the statute, as a member of what is called today an independent regulatory commission, were partly judicial (adjudicating complaints of unfair competition and acting on request as special master for a federal court) and partly legislative (implementing by orders and regulations a broad regulatory statute and submitting recommendations for legislation to Congress), as well as administrative in nature.

The Supreme Court in *Humphrey's Ex'r v. United States*, 295 U.S. 602, 55 S. Ct. 869, 79 L. Ed. 1611 (1935), held that the President had no inherent constitutional power to remove such an official in disregard of the provisions of the statute enacted by Congress fixing a term of office, since the commissioner's duties were not solely executive in nature.

103. Madison, JOURNAL, August 17.

104. FEDERALIST, No. 69.

105. FEDERALIST, No. 74.

106. James Wilson, a delegate to the Pennsylvania ratifying convention, described to the other delegates the principle that should control in drawing a line between the national government and the governments of the several states:

> Whatever object of government is confined, in its operation and effects, within the bounds of a particular state, should be considered as belonging to the government of that state; whatever object of government is confined, in its operation and effect, beyond the bounds of a particular state, should be considered as belonging to the government of the United States. But though this principle be sound and satisfactory, its application to particular cases would be accompanied with much difficulty, because, in its application, room must be allowed for great discretionary latitude of construction of the principle. In order to lessen or remove the difficulty arising from discretionary construction on this subject, an enumeration of particular instances, in which the application of the principle ought to take place, has been attempted with much industry and care.

J. Elliot, *Debates on the Federal Constitution*, Vol. 2 (Philadelphia: J.B. Lippincott Co. 1901), pp. 424–25; and see 443 ff. for an excellent comparison between powers under the Articles of Confederation and the Constitution.

107. See, e.g., Elliot, *Debates* Vol. 2, pp. 413–14 (The Circular Letter, from the Convention of the State of New York to the governors of the several States in the Union, July 28, 1788).

CHAPTER 4

108. M. Forkosh, CONSTITUTIONAL LAW 117 (Mineola, N.Y.: Foundation Press, 1963), referring to *Marbury v. Madison,* 5 U.S. (1 Cranch) 137, 2 L. Ed. 60 (1803).

109. E. Corwin, THE CONSTITUTION AND WHAT IT MEANS TODAY at xv (Princeton, N.J.: Princeton University Press, 1958).

110. 6 U.S. (2 Cranch) 169, 2 L. Ed. 243 (1804). In *Little,* captains were instructed by President John Adams to commandeer and take to American ports for condemnation all American vessels or those suspected to be American, even if they were authorized by foreign papers, when these ships were bound to or from French ports. An American commander captured a Danish ship, which had aroused his suspicions and which was sailing *from* a French port. However, the federal statute on which the President's order was based, relied upon by the vessel's owners, authorized stopping vessels owned by Americans when there was reason to suspect that they were engaged in traffic with France (with which nation a congressional act had suspended commercial intercourse) and were bound *for* France. Chief Justice Marshall expressed the opinion of the court that the President might have had the authority, in the absence of a statute, to stop the vessel in his capacity as the commander-in-chief who was executing the laws of the land as appropriate to conditions at that time. But he was deprived of any such authority because the statute specifically limited his control of craft that were voyaging *to* French ports. The Chief Justice said that the policy of this law obviously would be carried out with less evasion under the President's construction; however, "... the legislature seems to have prescribed that the manner in which this law shall be carried into execution, was to exclude a seizure of any vessel not bound to a French port...." The further context of the statute supported this conclusion. The court would have been willing to infer the President's power from his constitutional power to act as commander-in-chief, but it was not clear how far his authority in that capacity extended. The national legislature, as was seen in the preceding chaprter, itself had some overlapping powers; for example, the power to declare war, the power to appropriate funds with which to conduct a war, and other express rights. This created an overlapping power situation that Congress could settle. The first branch as the representative of the people can assign powers not expressly given to one of the other two branches as it sees fit. Under our constitutional system only the lawmaking body has this residual authority.

111. 143 U.S. 649 (1892). A delegation case antecedent to *Field* presented this question: If Congress enacts a law that will take effect provided a foreseen contingency actually occurs, is it delegating the lawmaking power to the second branch by empowering that branch to determine whether and when the condition happens, triggering the operation of the statute? This Supreme Court decision in 1813 dealt with a federal statute, adopted on the expiration date of an earlier

statute, and containing a provision that if either Great Britain or France, within the succeeding ten months, revoked its edicts that interfered with the neutrality of American commerce the President should issue a proclamation to this effect. Thereupon the country that had not revoked its edicts would have three additional months to do so; if it did not, *certain prohibitions in the expired statute* would be revived against it, but not against the first country, which had revoked its edict.

President Madison issued a proclamation on November 2, 1810, finding that France had revoked its edicts. On December 6, 1810, the brig *Aurora* set sail from Liverpool with goods destined for New Orleans, at which port the brig arrived a few days after February 2, 1811, the termination date of the waiting period. Great Britain had not revoked its edicts within the time prescribed in the act.

A federal district court condemned the cargo of the brig *Aurora*. The claimant of the goods raised the issue that Congress had no constitutional authority to delegate to the President, by a second statute, the power to revive provisions of an expired act of Congress. The Supreme Court, in an opinion written by Mr. Justice William Johnson, ruled against the claimant. It said that Congress could exercise its discretion conditionally, or expressly, "as their judgment should direct," namely, "upon the occurrence of any subsequent combination of events." *Cargo of the Brig Aurora v. United States,* 11 U.S. (7 Cranch) 382, 3 L. Ed. 380 (1813).

The Supreme Court refused to assume an overly technical position on whether a conditional law could be enacted; other than this its position was orthodox, since the legislature had firmly stated the policy directions for the executive to follow. To find an invalid delegation would have been to say that the legislature could not delegate such discretion as may be involved in the interpretations of edicts of foreign countries, a practice no doubt already being carried on in various connections as a matter of course within the executive establishment. As Professor Louis L. Jaffe has pointed out, no great exercise of administrative discretion was left to the President in this case; the question of delegation was not serious. L. Jaffe, JUDICIAL CONTROL OF ADMINISTRATIVE ACTION 52 (Boston: Little, Brown & Co., 1965). The problem attains grave proportions only when too much administrative discretion is conferred, that is, if Congress failed to give the second branch principles or policies upon which to base the decision that the condition exists.

112. 276 U.S. 294 (1928). We may note that the case involved the power of taxation, which, being specifically given to Congress in the Constitution, is one of the primary legislative powers; yet the tribunal sustained the power delegated. The court said that a revenue measure was not unconstitutional because it also had the purpose of protecting domestic production in a field of changing conditions in which the inherent necessities of governmental coordination were clear. The extent and character of the coordination of the three branches must be fixed according to common sense. Analogy was made to the historic delegation of the power over discriminatory prices to the Interstate Commerce Commission, and

the Court noted that administrative fixing of tariff rates under a clear policy and plan established by Congress had been recognized as appropriate in the earlier case, *Field v. Clark* (n. 111, above). In the case of the Interstate Commerce Commission, rate fixing took place after a hearing had been extended to a public utility company. In this statute a hearing first was required to be provided by the Tariff Commission, indicating the care with which the delegated power must be used. A grant of broad power to the Executive thus may be justified upon a basis of necessity, as a common sense accommodation of the legislative power to complicated and constantly changing economic conditions, if the delegation is restricted by criteria or guidelines written into the statute as policies that the official must follow. In this context, it may be seen that the complexity of the subjects of statutory delegations had changed considerably from the time of the *Field* case (1892) to the post–World War I period of expanded industrialism of the *Hampton* case (1928), when the transition from a pioneer rural agricultural society to an urban industrial society was complete. What had not changed during this period was the standard of reasonableness itself, which always must remain fixed in the face of divergent application of standards. In the words of the late Harvard Dean Roscoe Pound (*Pound, What is Law?*, 47 W. VA. L. Q. 1, 6 [1941]): law, in its ideal element, is "the body of received, authoritative ideals. . . [that] comes at bottom to the picture of the social order of the time and place, the legal tradition as to what that social order is and so as to what is the purpose of social control. . . ."

The Supreme Court found that Congress had laid down a legal policy and established its own will as to the norms of tariff charges, but with provisos that set out guidelines for the Executive to follow as conditions change under circumstances foreseen by Congress. It is obvious that these guidelines are broad, but when they are examined it is plain that the statutory guidelines could only be satisfied through determination by the President, following a commission's (and his own) study of the facts. So long as this was done, as provided for, a path of consistency on the part of the administrator with the statutory guidelines would be possible, and this would effectuate the policy of the law directed by Congress. To permit the President to make a determination "insofar as he finds it practicable" does not confer unbridled discretion but recognizes that there will not be mathematical accuracy in the cost and equalization comparisons, while declaring the lawmakers' will that the objective comparison factors shall constitute the guiding policy and consideration.

This statute cannot be said to lack a statement of broad policies that furnish criteria for fact finding. It may be that since many of the investigative data relative to comparative costs and prices must be furnished from abroad, the administration of such a statute may require foreign service officers to be clearinghouses for much of the information, and perhaps all of it. They will have some trained personnel, presumably fewer in times of rigid budgeting. Many of the data, due to the press of business, may be taken from foreign newspapers and trade journals, and all of this information may not be tested and accurate. The statute proceeds on the ground that the rules of necessity require, for the execution of its policies, that the executive do only the best he can. The law recognizes this; in requiring compliance with the various standards, it adds the condition that the President find this to be "practicable." If such data as the differences in wages and costs of production cannot always be determined with certitude, the President must be guided by them so far as "he finds it practicable." To assist in developing factual accuracy and expert judgment, the Congress gave the President the aid of a Tariff Commission, which held hearings on the facts and made recommendations. In all of this there is no occasion for alarm that the separation of powers doctrine of the Constitution has been destroyed.

Perfection of the details of operation is not a necessary requirement for a proper statutory delegation. The establishment of a rule of conduct is. The Court seems clearly correct in concluding that all the details of a statute need not be set down so long as a rule is adopted for the Executive to follow, the public to observe, and the courts to review against.

A further proposition utilized by the Court is that a statute declaring the law may leave the details of the law for implementation by the executive. However, this is a vague test that, when employed without analysis, can be used to sustain nearly any rule or regulation or proclamation that the second branch might issue. Schwartz, *A Decade of Administrative Law: 1942-51*, 51 MICH. L. REV. 775, 781 (1953).

If this test is applied by courts that set forth reasons—not mere conclusions—it would seem to be quite similar to the "intelligible principle" test. We start with the question of whether the law has really been declared, subject only to the filling in of details. This leads to the question of whether a true rule of conduct has been set forth in the law. If it has been, the details, which well may consist of regulations expressing considerable judgment and discretion for enforcing this rule of conduct, may appropriately be supplied by the administrator under the constitutional provision bestowing upon the President the power to execute the law and the power to enforce the law.

113. Dissenting opinion of Mr. Justice Joseph Bradley, *Chicago, Milwaukee & St. Paul R.R. Co. v. Minnesota*, 134 U.S. 418, 10 S. Ct. 462, 33 L. Ed. 970, 983 (1890) (". . . when the Legislature declares that the charges shall be reasonable, or, which is the same thing, allows the common law rule to that effect to prevail, and leaves the matter there, then resort may be had to the courts to inquire judicially whether the charges are reasonable. . . .")

The Court affirmance of broad grants of legislative power in certain areas often relies upon ancient usage; for example, the charter power of *municipalities* to act according to the "general welfare," and historical recognition of powers exercised at an early period by towns in the United States and in Europe, which did "more to promote civilization than all other causes combined" and which are institutional with us. (Foster, *The Delegation of Legislative Power to Administrative*

Officers, 7 ILL. L. REV. 397 [1913]). History lies at the base of affirmance of large power vesting in public utility commissions; in 1691 the English Parliament gave broad carriage rate powers to justices of the peace. The Interstate Commerce Commission Act, prohibiting carriers from imposing unjust and unreasonable rates as determined by the Interstate Commerce Commission, is an express adoption by the national legislature of the principles of the common law on this topic. *Tift v. Southern Ry. Co.,* 123 F. 789, (C.C.S.D. Ga. 1903). *See also, I.C.C. v. Baltimore & Ohio Ry. Co.,* 145 U.S. 263, 36 L. Ed. 699, 705 (1891); *McDonald v. Hovey,* 110 U.S. 619, 28 A.L.R. 269 (1884).

Professor Jaffe says, in *An Essay on Delegation of Legislative Power,* 47 Col. L. Rev. 350, 560 (1947):

> It is usually argued that nothing can be vaguer than the delegation to act in the "public interest." But as the Court pointed out in the New York Central Securities case (*New York Central Securities Corp. v. United States,* 287 U.S. 12, 53 S. Ct. 45, 77 L. Ed. 138 [1932]), a power to allow consolidation or new construction when in "the public interest" implies the criteria of adequacy of service, of economy and efficiency as those concepts have been developed in the specific context of the railroad industry. . . . [E]ven the power to prescribe "just and reasonable rates" has in the past, at least, expressly or impliedly referred to a concept of ratemaking, in certain cases a "fair" return on a "rate base," in others out-of-pocket costs. It is true that in the Hope Natural Gas case, *FPC v. Hope Natural Gas Co.,* 320 U.S. 59, 64 S. Ct. 281, 88 L. Ed. 333 (1944), the Court more or less disregarded the apparent direction to the FPC to proceed in the light of the traditional concept. . . . But Justice Douglas . . . does state that from the investor or company point of view it is important that there be enough revenue not only for operating expenses but also for the capital costs of the business. These include service on the debt and dividends on the stock. By that standard the return to the equity owner should be commensurate with returns on investments in other enterprises having corresponding risks. That return, moreover, should be sufficient to assure confidence in the financial integrity of the enterprise, so as to maintain its credit and to attract capital.
>
> Here is a fairly precise guide in fixing minimum if not maximum rates; and it is meant to operate in a field where there is at least a central core of agreement on the methods to be followed in achieving such results. . . . But were a commission in a borderline case to use none of the basic methods of evaluating investment and fair return and to speculate entirely in terms of the capacity to attract new capital, a very different opinion may be written. . . ."

114. In *Federal Trade Commission v. Gratz*, 253 U.S. 421, 40 S. Ct. 572, 64 L. Ed. 933 (1920), the Court held that the statutory words of grant to the Commission of the power to restrain "unfair methods of competition" were inexact and undefined by the statute; therefore what practices the words included were for the Court, and not the Commission, to determine. "The act was certainly not intended to fetter free and fair competition as commonly understood and practised by honorable opponents in trade." 253 U.S. at 428, 64 L. Ed. at 996. Since the power to determine the illegal practice remained with the courts and was not delegated to the Commission, no question of unlawful delegation of legislative power existed. The determination of the Commission is entitled to weight at the hands of the Court. *FTC v. R.F. Keppel & Bros.*, 291 U.S. 304, 314, 54 S. Ct. 423, 78 L. Ed. 814, 820 (1934).

115. 12 U.S.C. § 1464 (d).

116. *Fahey v. Malonee*, 332 U.S. 245, 67 S. Ct. 1552, 91 L. Ed. 2030.

117. See notes 110–113.

118. 289 U.S. 266, 53 S. Ct. 627, 77 L. Ed. 1166 (1933).

119. See, e.g., *New York Central Securities Corp. v. United States*, 287 U.S. 12, 24, 53 S. Ct. 45, 77 L. Ed. 138 (1932); and *Amalgamated Meat Cutters v. Connally*, 337 F. Supp. 737 (D.D.C. 1971). *See also*, Marshall, J., concurring in *National Cable Television Ass'n. v. United States*, 415 U.S. 336 (1974); *Environmental Defense Fund v. Ruckelshaus*, 439 F. 2d 584 (D.C. Cir. 1971); *Iske v. United States*, 396 F.2d 28, 31 (10th Cir. 1968); 1 Davis, Ad. L. Text §§ 2.03, 2.04, 2.05, 2.08, 2.15 (1972). *Compare*, Jaffe, *An Essay on Delegation of Legislative Power* 47 Col. L. Rev. 350 (1947), J. Skelly Wright, *Beyond Discretionary Justice*, 81 Yale L.J. 575 (1972); *United States v. Robel*, 389 U.S. 258, 276 (1967) (Brennan, J., concurring in the result); Merrill, *Standards—A Safeguard for the Exercise of Delegated Power* 47 Nebr. L. Rev. 469 (1968).

120. 334 U.S. 742, 68 S. Ct. 1294, 92 L. Ed. 1694 (1948). Another World War II decision may be noted. It related to the indispensability to the actual fighting of the war, of maintaining the stability of our economy. In furtherance of this need, the Emergency Price Control Act of 1942 was adopted. The purpose of the Act was declared to be "to stabilize prices . . . to eliminate . . . profiteering . . . to assure that defense appropriations are not dissipated by excessive prices; to protect persons with relatively fixed and limited incomes . . . to prevent a post emergency collapse of values. . . ." A federal administrator was provided to administer this statute.

The standards governing his administration were as follows. He was given power to fix prices that "in his judgment will be generally fair and equitable and will effectuate the purposes of this Act." The Administrator was required "so far as practicable" to "give due consideration" to prices prevailing on dates designated in the statute, and by a later statute he was directed to stabilize prices "so far as practicable" on the basis of levels of a later date. His powers extended under the statute to determine the prices of individual commodities, rents, and services in order "to stabilize prices and to prevent speculative, unwarranted, and abnormal increases in prices and rents." The first statutory reference point to prices prevailing on designated dates was to prices between October 1 and October 15, 1941. (These dates were changed by amendments in later years.) The Administrator was authorized to make adjustments in this formula to reflect increases or decreases in costs and profits. Finally he was required by statute to set out a "statement of the considerations" involved in his establishment of varying ceilings for prices and rents.

The delegation of power to the Administrator was placed in question in *Yakus v. United States*, 321 U.S. 414, 64 S. Ct. 660, 88 L. Ed. 834 (1944). *Yakus* involved an appeal of a conviction for the sale of beef above the maximum price that had been fixed by the Administrator. The delegation was upheld.

The Court noted the fact that this was a statute in aid of the war, though it laid less emphasis upon the war power than it later did in the *Lichter* case, above.

The Court said that Congress had stated the legislative objective, maximum price fixing, and had laid down standards to guide the administrative determination of both the occasion for the exercise of the price-fixing power and the particular prices to be established.

Obviously broad discretion was vested by this statute in the Administrator. First, the area of regulatory control was extensive. Second, the standard, "generally fair and equitable," while helpful, was vague. But third, and highly important, was the requirement in the statute that the Administrator give "due consideration," "so far as practicable," to prices as they existed during stipulated periods.

It might be speculated that when an administrator is enjoined by statute to give "due consideration" to a stated congressional policy, the result is the same as when no policy is stated at all: that the administrator can give "due consideration" by merely paying momentary attention to the statutory factor and then moving arbitrarily in an entirely different direction. However, in practice and in law this speculation would be ill-founded. The administrator realizes that the factor so stated is substantially controlling, though Congress deliberately gives him latitude for occasions when following such a factor would prove impracticable and would reach an unfair and inequitable result. The long and short of this is that there is an expression of will and of policy by the Congress, though one so general that grave questions might be raised as to its validity if the delegation were conferred in peace time when the nature of the subject matter and of the necessity should require less administrative latitude.

In 1970, with one political party in control of the White House and the other in control of the Congress, a very brief provision was inserted in a series of amendments to the Defense Production Act of 1950 (50 U.S.C. Appendix §§ 2061–2168 [1970]) giving the President authority to stabilize prices and wages, among other things, without expectation that he would use the power. In 1971, the President issued Executive Order No. 11615 (36 Fed. Reg. 15727), thereby using the authority granted. He limited the effective period to ninety days.

The standards in the statute are not easy to find: the statute is permissive, not directory; does not mention a war purpose; and grants authority "to issue such orders and regulations as he may deem appropriate to stabilize prices, rents, wages, and salaries *at levels not less than those prevailing on May 25, 1970.*" (Underscoring added.) The *underscored* provision constitutes a fairly definite standard, at least insofar as a minimum requirement is concerned, but it seems to stand alone and therefore to be inadequate to guide administrative exercise of discretion unless a standard can be found in the final language: "Such orders . . . may provide for the making of such adjustments as may be necessary to prevent gross inequities." (12 U.S.C. § 1904, note, quoting Title II of P.L. 91-379, Aug. 15, 1970, 84 Stat. 799, 201-206 as amended by P.L. 91-558 [1970], P.L. 92-8 [1971].) This is exceedingly broad terminology.

The 1970 statute was revised in 1971, adding in considerable detail to the above provision, following a decision by the U.S. Court of Appeals for the District of Columbia Circuit. (P.L. 92-210, Dec. 22, 1971, 40 L.W. 35.)

An article in the Duke Law Journal (*Project Federal Administrative Law Development—1971, 1972,* Duke L.J. 115, 135-36, hereinafter cited as *Duke* gives a good analysis of the above case of *Amalgamated Meat Cutters v. Connally,* 337 Federal Supp. 737 (D.D.C. 1971) (three-judge district court), wherein the President's action and the 1970 statute were sustained on narrow grounds. The Court limited its approval to the *temporary* action of the President in imposing a ninety-day freeze; it noted that the failure in the law to state the goals to be achieved was compensated for by legislative history evidenced in congressional committee reports; it gave consideration to the price control legislation enacted during World War II, and the agency actions and court decisions thereunder, as context that Congress intended to be used by the Executive Branch to clarify the more vaguely drafted 1970 act. It also found that the Act narrowed the President's discretion somewhat, insofar as one amendatory provision prohibited "stabilization" of a particular industry unless predicated upon a finding that wages and prices had risen disproportionately in that industry. (*Duke* at 131.)

In the article's view the Court was forced to strain to reach its decision, which is quite true. If so broad and vague a delegation is sustainable, perhaps the pragmatic reason is the best: the power was limited to a ninety-day period. However, this is a pragmatic choice unsupported by legal reasoning.

121. FEDERALIST No. 23.
122. 92 L. Ed. 1694, 1725.
123. 276 U.S. 394, 48 S. Ct. 348, 72 L. Ed. 624 (1928).
124. 299 U.S. 304, 57 S. Ct. 216, 81 L. Ed. 255 (1936).
125. Id., at 324, 223, and 265, respectively.
126. 468 U.S. _____ , 82 L. Ed. 2d 171, 104 S. Ct. 3026 (1984).
127. Id., at 187.
128. 381 U.S. 1, 85 S. Ct. 1271, 14 L. Ed. 2d 179 (1965).
129. 43 Col L. Rev. 213, 214 (1943).

130. 220 U.S. 506, 31 S. Ct. 480, 55 L. Ed. 563 (1911).

131. It is upon this ground that the holding of the Supreme Court in 1963 in the case of *Arizona v. California,* 337 U.S. 546, 83 S. Ct. 1468, 10 L. Ed. 2d 542, seems sustainable. The Interior Department was delegated broad power to allocate water to several claimant states from the Colorado River, a navigable stream and hence under control of the United States, in times of water shortage. The congressional directions were to allocate according to priorities: (1) river regulation and flood control; (2) irrigation and domestic uses and satisfaction of present perfected right to use the flow; and (3) power production. The Supreme Court said in part, over the objection of three dissenters who regarded the statute as unrestrained delegation, "Congress still has broad powers over this navigable international stream. . . . [W]e leave in the hands of the Secretary, where Congress has placed it, full power to control, manage and operate the Government's Colorado River works and to make contracts for the sale and delivery of water on such terms as are not prohibited by the Project Act." It may be noted that Congress did not leave the power to allocate to the complete discretion of the secretary under a vague "public interest" standard; it required him to allocate in accordance with priority standards it set forth. They were broad but not unconfined. The special constitutional power of Congress over navigable waters of the United States (*Coyle v. Smith,* 55 L. Ed. 853, 860 [U.S. 1910]) may be compared to the proprietary interest in the national forests referred to, causing the courts to be more sympathetic to the otherwise excessively general standards reviewed in *Arizona v. California.*

132. See K. DAVIS, DISCRETIONARY JUSTICE: A PRELIMINARY INQUIRY (Baton Rouge: Louisiana State Univ. Press, 1969).

133. Austern, *The Problem of Food Standards,* PROCEEDINGS OF THE ASSOCIATION OF AMERICAN LAW SCHOOLS, 1962–64, 209.

See also, J. FitzGerald, *Adoption of Federal Power Commission Price Changing Rules without Evidentiary Hearing: Statutory Collision,* 18 Sw. L.J. 236, 268–71 (1964).

As stated in Fairlie, *Administrative Legislation,* 18 Mich. L. Rev. 181, 197 (1920), quoting the case of *United States v. Louisville Ry. Co.,* 176 F. 942 (1910):

> A crime may only be created, by a public act, the language of which act is sufficient in itself to completely declare and define the crime and fix its punishment. Congress having no power to delegate . . . authority to declare what facts shall constitute an offense, though it is competent . . . to commit to the executive the power to determine when the occasion provided by the law itself . . . has occurred. . . .

However, "the determination of guilt in criminal prosecutions can never be committed to other than judicial officers." (Powell, *Separation of Powers,* 27 Pol.

Sci. Q. 215, 235 [1913].) Professor Powell quotes from *Wong Wing v. United States*, 163 U.S. 228 (1896): "... It is not consistent with the theory of our government that the legislature should, after having defined an offence as an infamous crime, find the fact of guilt and adjudge the punishment by one of its own agents."

The imposition of money penalties is held not necessarily penal in nature. (Powell, *Separation of Powers*, 235.)

    134. 294 U.S. 295, 55 S. Ct. 837, 79 L. Ed. 1570 (1935).

    135. Act of June 16, 1933, 15 U.S.C. § 703.

    136. 79 L. Ed. at 1576–77; 15 U.S.C. § 701.

    137. Id., at 1581, note 9.

    138. Earlier in the same year that the Supreme Court decided the *Schechter* case, it decided the case of *Panama Refining Co. v. Ryan*, 293 U.S. 388, 55 S. Ct. 241, 79 L. Ed. 446 (1935). *Schechter* was a unanimous opinion of the court; in *Panama*, Mr. Justice Cardozo dissented. In both, the statute involved was held unconstitutional for the same reason.

Panama involved an injunction proceeding brought by the owner of an oil plant in Texas to prevent federal and state officials from enforcing by criminal prosecution Section 9 (c) of the National Industrial Act (15 U.S.C. § 709[c]) and an Executive Order of the President issued under the act, approving a Petroleum Code the effect of which was to bar the plaintiff from shipping oil in interstate commerce.

Under Section 9(c), the President was

> authorized to prohibit the transportation in interstate or foreign commerce of petroleum or the products thereof produced or withdrawn from storage in excess of the amount permitted to be drawn by any State law or valid regulation or order prescribed thereunder.

Criminal penalties were provided for violations of the President's orders.

The President exercised his authority by promulgating an executive order in which he outlawed, from interstate and foreign commerce, petroleum and petroleum products that were produced in excess of "any State law or valid regulation or order prescribed thereunder, by any board, commission, officer, or other duly authorized agency of a State...." (293 U.S. at 405, 406, 79 L. Ed. 451.)

The Court first held that since the President was merely authorized to prohibit such transportation he had full choice whether to apply the will of Congress or not, and therefore no will of Congress was expressed. It further held that the legislative policy under this provision of the Act was left "to the States and to their constituted authorities" without any criterion to guide the President whatsoever. The Court found that the President had unfettered discretion to enforce or not enforce (by barring shipment of the excess products in interstate commerce and prosecuting violations) the regulations of states prohibiting excessive amounts of their petroleum resources from being produced; or he could simply exercise the discretion not to act at all. No standard or limitation was contained in the statute to determine what would be excessive production. This was left to the discretion of the states, the Congress thus authorizing the President to adopt for the future, by prohibitions criminally enforceable, under the commerce power, laws, regulations, or orders of states and their officials, which actions in many cases had not yet been taken and the character of which therefore was not known.

The argument was made by the government that the President's discretion was limited by the declarations of policy in the early part of the statute, the breadth of which has been discussed in relation to the *Schechter* case. However, the Supreme Court said that Section 9 (c) was distinct and separate from the earlier declarations of policy and therefore stood on its own; further, that the declarations were purely an introduction to the Act and stated no legislative policy.

Mr. Justice Cardozo dissented in this case. He believed that the statute should be upheld as a proper delegation on the theory that the President's apparent unlimited option under Section 9 (c) in fact was given mandatory direction by Section 1—the section setting out mandatory but indefinite policy objectives discussed above in the review of the *Schechter* case.

A comparison with a much more recent federal law may be of interest. The National Labor Relations Act today permits bargaining over union shop agreements, which require workers to become members of a union (if it becomes the recognized bargaining agent) within a short period of time after entering on their employment; but the Act withdraws that permission if a state has a law that forbids union shop agreements. Thus the Congress expresses its will that union shop clauses are valid from a federal point of view, but it recognizes that the matter is a debatable issue of state policy, and it forbids such clauses in collective bargaining agreements made in states prohibiting them. The contrast should be noticed with the *Panama* delegation. In *Panama* the President could issue an executive order or refrain from doing so as he saw fit. The states could regulate this natural resource or not; those that did not thereby gave the President no option to adopt a code effective as to them; but he had that option notwithstanding that a state determined to regulate. The proposed national pattern of regulation under the statute therefore could be most checkered. In *Panama*, if he issued such an order he would close interstate channels to petroleum products produced beyond quotas established by a given state; in another state establishing its own quotas the President could elect not to close interstate channels. Thus he might very well be closing interstate channels to states that produced very little petroleum and leaving interstate channels free for use of states producing excessive petroleum. It would appear that both the majority and Mr. Justice Cardozo in dissent saw this complete absence of rational connection between authorized Presidential action and federal use of the commerce power. Cardozo sought to meet the problem by relying on the general declarations of policy that were commented on in connection with the preceding case. The majority said they did not apply, and in any event had no more force than a preface or introduction to the statute. In any case, from the subsequent degree of rigor that the Supreme Court has exercised in reviewing broad delegations to the Executive Branch since *Panama,* it appears that Theodore W. Cousens said it all very accurately back in 1935:

> It is obvious, however, that those who look to the Supreme Court for protection against extensive delegations to the Executive should not take too much confidence from this decision. No substantial barrier to delegation is voiced by the Panama Refining Co. case. A standard must be set, but previous cases teach how vague such a standard may be and there is certainly nothing here irreconcilable with those cases. The Court has indeed set a limit, but it is formal rather than substantial and the slightest care in drafting will avoid infringing it. All in all, we may conclude that the case changes nothing and that its importance can very easily be exaggerated. Cousens, *The Delegation of Federal Legislative Power to Executive Officials,* 33 Mich. L. Rev. 512, 544 (1935).

This is a realistic appraisal of what the Supreme Court has done in later cases and more generally what the lower federal courts of appeal and district courts have done; but it is not necessarily to be considered an appraisal of the practice the federal judiciary should have followed. In *Panama* there was a basic problem: Should the President be delegated the power without standards to determine if a law should ever go into effect? The President could act to stop hot oil shipments that were contrary to state law, but he need not take action or act selectively without good reason. Hence he could negate the very policy the law was supposedly announcing.

This basic defect was repeated in the Price Control Act of 1970, as appears elsewhere, leaving to the unbridled discretion of the President, in the 1970 Act, without reference to any standards to determine the occurrence of the contingency, whether to apply wage and price controls to the nation's economy. Few broader areas of legislative or executive conduct could be imagined. As has been seen, President Nixon took a deliberate approach, placing controls into effect for only ninety days while he could request and obtain from Congress a more definite statement of legislative policy, which he secured.

139. Several of the decisions are noted in C. Pritchett, THE AMERICAN CONSTITUTION 201–203 (New York: McGraw Hill Book Co., 2d ed. 1968).Illustrations listed are *Currin v. Wallace,* 306 U.S. 1, 59 S. Ct. 379, 83 L. Ed. 441 (1939); *United*

States v. Rock Royal Cooperative, 307 U.S. 533, 59 S. Ct. 993, 83 L. Ed. 1146 (1939); and *Hood & Sons v. United States,* 307 U.S. 588, 59 S. Ct. 1019, 83 L. Ed. 1478 (1939)--all upholding the Federal Tobacco Inspection Act and the Agricultural Marketing Agreement Act.

See also the extremely permissive delegation referred to by Pritchett in *United States v. Sharpnack,* 355 U.S. 286 (1958). This decision of the Supreme Court upheld a 1948 act making *future state laws,* as well as existing state laws, applicable to minor criminal offenses on federal enclaves (such as Army or Air Force bases). Justices William O. Douglas and Hugo Black, both liberal advocates of the administrative process and slow to question broad delegations normally, dissented on the basis of *Schechter* case.

Pritchett goes on to suggest the following guides for appropriate limitations upon the power of Congress to delegate authority to the Executive: Congress must define the subject of the delegation and provide a recognizable standard or criterion to guide the agent to whom legislative powers are delegated; where contingent legislation is involved, a definite finding with respect to the contingency specified in the statute must be made; legislative power must be delegated only to public officials, not to private persons or organizations; finally, Congress must itself provide any penal sanctions for the violation of administrative legislation.

140. A large number of law review articles accept as adequate standards ones that are subject to question, supporting such acceptance by broad conclusions that the "complexities of the situation," rapidly changing conditions and times, or social progress so require. For examples, *see* C.W. Daby, *A New View of Delegation of Powers,* 18 U. Cin. L. Rev. 484 (1949); Note, 4 St. Louis U.L.J. 79 (1956); Parker, *The Historic Basis of Administrative Law: Separation of Powers and Judicial Supremacy,* 12 Rutgers L. Rev. 449 (1958). A number of courts follow this approach also or apply such conclusions as makeweights after undertaking an analysis of the statute, and it would appear that some writers and courts may be unduly concerned that an attack upon a statute based on the nondelegation doctrine in reality is an attack upon social change. Concluding that there has been a definite swing away from the *Panama* and *Schechter* cases, Professor Schwartz, in *A Decade of Administrative Law: 1942-1951* (51 Mich. L. Rev. 775, 782 [1953]), sadly reflects that the "requirements of standards in the federal field has become more a matter of form than of substance."

141. Merrill, *Standards—A Safeguard for the Exercise of Delegated Power,* 47 Neb. L. Rev. 469 (1968). Ralph F. Fuchs, also a leading administrative law scholar, referred to this article in his essay, *Maurice H. Merrill's Contribution to Administrative Law,* 25 Okla. L. Rev. 490, 494 (1972), as "a discussion of constitutional standards governing the delegation of broad discretionary authority, which in my judgment is the best treatment this subject has received...."

Merrill's article argues the necessity for adequate standards in statutes delegating powers to administrative agencies. A substantial part of his article is devoted to demonstrating that there are a number of kinds of standards that may qualify as adequate. His classifications follow.

1. Standards that prescribe specific and objective tests against which the action taken is to be tried. Thus a law may direct a licensing board that it may revoke a license if the licensee has been convicted in a court of competent jurisdiction of a crime.

2. A "reasonably detailed portraiture of legislative purpose." In this class Merrill places a delegation to the Secretary of the Treasury to prescribe "[u]niform standards of purity, quality and fitness for consumption of all kinds of teas imported into the United States." The dominant concept is that admissible tea shall be fit for human consumption, "a not unmanageable idea." He also places in this category delegations that are worded in terms of the "public interest," but other language in the statute makes this term sufficiently objective and sufficiently precise, for example, a sufficiently detailed specification of particular factors that are to be considered administratively prior to determining where the public interest lies.

3. An imprecise standard applied to limited subject matter; for example, a delegation of authority to the Internal Revenue Service to prescribe the books and records to be kept by a taxpayer, or a delegation to the Federal Communications Commission to prescribe the books and records to be kept by a telegraph or telephone company engaged in interstate commerce. There is no precise definition of the books and records to be kept, but the narrow area of operation of the subject indicates with sufficient certainty what kinds of books and records the administrator would require. Thus, in the case of the Internal Revenue Service, such books and records will facilitate the determination of liability and collection of the revenue. Another example is the power to make regulations concerning the use of federal forest reserves, noted above in connection with the *Grimaud* case. Here the power is limited by the objects of the forest reserve, which is a rather limited matter when compared with the revival of the national economy, dealt with in *Schechter,* or the protection of collective bargaining.

4. Imprecise words acquiring legal significance include the delegation of power to a regulating body to approve reasonable rates for gas or electric service. The word "reasonable" is extremely broad. However, as has been indicated earlier in this chapter, the word has for centuries been judicially construed, and its meaning thus has been defined. It may be presumed Congress is using the term in the light of its judicially defined meaning.

5. "Imprecise words aided by analogous statutes" is a term for a situation in which a broad statute under consideration may be construed by reference to an analogous statute upon some independent but related subject in order to discover the object that the lawmakers "wish administrators to accomplish." The *Lichter* excess profits case, discussed above, would qualify.

6. Imprecise words that are made specific by administrative action would compose the type of broad statutory standard that is applied subject to required procedures, and with resort to judicial review stipulated. Apparently also included would be statutory delegations of power that through such a procedural

process have been interpreted by administrative action from time to time and these interpretations absorbed into the law over a period of years. This kind of classification, Merrill concedes, is a "bootstrap operation," although he believes that it permits broad statutory language to be sharpened through the adversary process and through opportunity to the parties to make their case and learn the reasons for actions for or against them. Merrill sees some merit in permitting this kind of classification to qualify as a standard. However, without deprecating the precedential value of such required procedure, some will have difficulty in overlooking its bootstrap origin unless and until with the passage of time this standard merits qualification under Merrill's classification 4.

7. In view of the extremely specific powers granted to the President in the category of national self-preservation—that is, war powers and foreign relations—more liberal approval of broad statutory delegations has been the rule. Merrill believes that judges and commentators often fail to appreciate the value of requiring statutory delegations to observe the "standards" doctrine because they "do not pay sufficient attention to the analysis of the grounds upon which standards may be sustained," namely, the classifications he has suggested. Further, the tendency of the courts is to say that a statute declares the legislative policy, and thus meets the requirements of the nondelegation doctrine and of due process. The courts could provide a distinct service if they would assume the additional analytical burden of considering whether, and explaining why, the "standards" used in the statute are reasonable.

142. See note 119.

143. In part, these reasons are drawn from Professor Frank E. Cooper, in 1 Cooper, State Administrative Law 74–91 (1965.)

144. *Arizona v. California*, 373 U.S. 546, 625–27, 83 S. Ct. 1468, 10 L. Ed. 2d 542, 603, 604 (1963).

145. From an unpublished 1964 writing of the late Professor Frank E. Cooper, reproduced with the consent of Margaret Cooper. Frank Cooper was one of the most thoughtful scholars, productive authors, and successful practitioners in the history of Administrative Law in the United States. He was the author of a unique two-volume treatise, STATE ADMINISTRATIVE LAW, and other books on Administrative Law and Legal Writing. Professor Cooper served as executive director of the Hoover Commission Task Force on reorganizing and improving the structure of the administrative branch and as chairman of the Administrative Law Section of the American Bar Association.

146. *Pennsylvania v. Nelson*, 350 U.S. 497 (1956).

147. As stated by George E. Atkinson, Jr., in a report of the ABA Administrative Law Section's Housing and Urban Development Committee, to which he contributed as vice-chairman, *Annual Report of Committee*, 4 A.B.A. Sec. Ad. L. Rev. 72 (1967):

"When the rule of Federal 'Preemption' of State laws is coupled with vague and indefinite delegations of power in the language of the preempting Federal statutes, the result with increasing frequency is to terminate State control of state affairs due to unguided or arbitrary actions of Federal administrators, substituting Federal sovereignty for State sovereignty.

"In a federal circuit court case in 1935 the city had entered into agreement with the federal government whereby the federal government would finance the bonds of the city for the purpose of building a municipal power facility. The plaintiff, whose existing business would suffer economic harm due to the competition of the city, challenged the extensive provisions in the government loan agreement that regulated the type of work force to be employed, the manner and amount of payment of wages, and the construction materials to be used. The Court struck down the agreement, saying:

A legislative power granted to a municipal corporation cannot be parted with unless such was the clear intent of the legislature, for it will never be presumed that the legislature, having granted the power, has at the same time authorized the surrender of it. The authority to surrender the power must appear from the "clear letter of the law" . . .

"Were it not for the fact that the United States is financing the project, we do not believe that it would even be suggested that a city could enter into any such arrangement with a lender of money, a buyer of bonds, or even a giver of gifts. . . . The relation of the United States to the city is no different than would be the relation to it of an individual, or corporation.

"It is apparent that, while the government was willing to finance the city, it insisted upon retaining sufficient control over plans, construction contracts, labor and materials, to ensure that the money furnished would be spent in the way the government thought it should be spent, whether that was in accord with the ideas of the city council or not." *Arkansas-Missouri Power Co. v. City of Kennett,* 78 F.2d. 911, 921–923 (8th Cir. 1935).

148. 29 Okla. L. Rev. 577 (1976).
149. 386 U.S. 670, 87 S. Ct. 1244, 18 L. Ed. 2d 395 (1967).
150. *Myers v. United States,* 272 U.S. 106, 71 L. Ed. 160, 166 (1926).
151. Remarks, "Committee Veto: Fifty Years of Sparring between the Executive and the Legislature," by Hon. William H. Rehnquist, then Assistant Attorney General, Office of Legal Counsel, before the Section of Administrative Law of the American Bar Association, Dallas, Texas, August 12, 1969. See also, 1 ANNALS OF CONGRESS 581.

152. Mendelson, *Jefferson on Judicial Review, Consistency through Change,* 29 U. CHICAGO L. REV. 327 (1962).

153. Remarks, "Separation of Powers--Rebirth of a Constitutional Principle?" by Lawrence H. Baskir, former chief counsel and staff director of the Subcommittee on Separation of Powers, U.S. Senate, before the Administrative Law Section, American Bar Association, Dallas, Texas, August 12, 1969.

154. Note 150 offers an example.

155. Duff & Whiteside, *Delegata Potestas Non Potest Delegari: A Maxim of American Constitutional Law,* 14 CORNELL L. Q. 168 (1928).

156. Jaffe, *An Essay on Delegation of Legislative Power,* 47 COLUM. L. REV. 561, 563 (1947).

157. Jaffe, *An Essay on Delegation of Legislative Power* 563.

158. *United States v. Enmons,* 410 U.S. 396, 413, 418, 93 S. Ct. 1007, 1016, 1019, 35 L. Ed. 2d. 379, 390, 393 (1973) (Douglas, J., dissenting).

CHAPTER 5

159. C. Zinn, *How Our Laws Are Made,* Document No. 125, 90th Cong., 1st Sess. (1967), pp. 3-4.

160. The recently created Office of Legislative and Intergovernmental Affairs in the Department of Justice, headed by an assistant attorney general, performs functions for the department generally similar in respect to proposed federal legislation to those performed by the general counsel of a government department, independent commission, or administrative agency.

The department's organizational regulations provide 28 CFR § 0.27 (Order No. 504-73, 38 F.R. 6893, March 14, 1973, as amended):

> The Assistant Attorney General in charge of the Office of Legislative and Intergovernmental Affairs is responsible for liaison between the Department and Congress, State and local governments, and related interest groups. The Office prepares reports and recommendations with respect to pending legislation originating in the Department of Justice or elsewhere in the Government. The Office coordinates all departmental efforts to advise the Congress on departmental views and to secure enactment of the Department's legislative agenda.
>
> The Office also alerts officials of State and local governments and related interest groups to significant departmental policy decisions, encourages dialog with interested officials, and solicits consultation on program issues and policies which fall within the responsibility of the Department.

The office's responsibilities are perhaps more numerous than those of most senior attorneys in charge of similar functions for administrative agencies, since the department administers a variety of statutes, from those dealing with criminal and civil litigation to those relating to immigration and land and natural resources. And, there are occasions when the White House may wish a policy objective implemented with respect to another existing department or new executive agency to be created for the purpose. This office may furnish such legislative drafting assistance as required on behalf of the attorney general, though that is unlikely if the program objective has been formulated into a legislative proposal by another cabinet department through its Office of General Counsel. Since the primary legislative function is coordinating the preparation of proposed departmental legislation within the Department of Justice, the actual drafting of the latter proposals desired for the functional purposes of an office of the department, such as the Land and Natural Resources or the Anti-Trust Division, would presumably occur in these initiating divisions.

161. See Executive Office of the President, Office of Management and Budget, Circular No. A-19, 5 C.F.R. chap. 3, p. 66 (rev. July 31, 1971).

162. Zinn, *How Our Laws Are Made.*

163. 2 U.S.C. § 190a(a), (b).

164. Id., § 190a-1 (a), (b).

165. The Cordon Rule requires that every bill being reported out of committee show the existing law as it would be modified by the bill, by italicizing all new material being reported out in the bill.

166. 2 U.S.C. § 190a(c).

167. There is a difference between the House and Senate in clearing legislation to the floor: the House rules of procedure limit individual members in offering amendments to bills that reach the floor for debate. This limitation is based upon the conditions for debate that the Rules Committee in the House lays down with particular reference to whether amendments can be offered to a bill after it comes to the floor. In the Senate a bill for all practical purposes may be rewritten on the floor due to the freedom of individual senators to offer amendments. The House Rules Committee, however, can and does attach conditions to clearance that prohibit introduction of an amendment to the bill unless the amendment is specifically identifiable and its content already known by notice to the Rules Committee.

168. Zinn, *How Our Laws Are Made,* pp. 19–23.

169. U.S.C., §§ 272, 282 a-e. In the Senate appointment is by the President pro tempore, 2 U.S.C. § 272.

170. J. Moore, *Foreword to the Office of Legislative Counsel,* 29 COL. L. REV. 379, 380 (1929).

171. Congressional Record, Dec. 10, 1969, at S16298-99: Statement of Senator Jordan (D., N.C.), Chairman of the Senate Committee on Rules and Administration, in recognition of the Fiftieth Anniversary of the Office of Legislative Counsel.

172. 2 U.S.C. § 281a.

173. 2 U.S.C. § 288.

174. 2 U.S.C. § 166.

175. 5 U.S.C. §§ 500–503, 551–559, 701–706 (1977).

176. *Immigration and Naturalization Service v. Chadha*, 77 L. Ed. 2d 317, 462 U.S. 919, 103 S. Ct. 2764 (1983). Justice Byron R. White, in dissent, stressed the long history of legislative veto usage and argued that the legislative veto power is not the power to write new law without bicameral approval or presidential consideration: "The vote must be authorized by statute and may only negative what an Executive department or independent agency has proposed. On its face, the legislative veto no more allows one House of Congress to make law than does the presidential veto confer such power upon the President. . . ." The justice referred to constitutional history; M. FARRAND, THE RECORDS OF THE FEDERAL CONVENTION OF 1787, Vol. II, pp. 301–302, 304–305; and ELLIOT, DEBATES, Vol. 5, p. 431, in support of his contention that the ". . . Framers were concerned with limiting the methods of enacting new legislation . . ." (77 L. Ed. 2d 363–64).

The dissenting opinion also made the reasonable point that ". . . [i]f Congress may delegate lawmaking power to independent and executive agencies, it is most difficult to understand Article I as forbidding Congress from also reserving a check on legislative power for itself . . ." (Id., 367).

Insofar as the action of the court of appeals is concerned that struck § 244 (c) (2), of the statute as violating the separation of powers principle, Mr. Justice White considers the past Court decisions as entirely to the contrary, and makes the unfortunate statement (id., 375) that ". . . [t]he separation of powers doctrine has heretofore led to the invalidation of government action only when the challenged action violated some express provision in the Constitution. . . ." The cases cited all deal with congressionally imposed restrictions upon executive power, but had been introduced by a decision approving a delegation of power to he president (*Hampton & Co. v. U.S.*, referred to in note 109). The statement also takes no account of *Schechter v. U.S.* (note 135).

The justices's argument with respect to bicameralism is telling, unless we wish to consider all strictly administrative acts to be of the same constitutional quality as acts of Congress. It would seem that the Court might more appropriately have rested its opinion upon separation of powers grounds, since the interference with administration seems to be evident in routine congressional exercise of veto power upon administrative orders generally. Judicial designation of all such orders as legislation, subject to presidential veto power, on the other hand, seems to involve strained reasoning.

177. As a recognized authority has indicated, in modern times the "executive communication" (or administratively drafted bill) is the chief type of bill considered by Congressional Committees. Zinn, *How Our Laws Are Made*, pp. 3–4, 6.

178. John Austin, *Lectures on Jurisprudence, or the Philosophy of Positive Law* (4th ed., 1873) 1136, cited by F. Lee in his article, *The Office of the Legislative Counsel,* 29 COL. L. REV. 381, 403 (1929). Lee quoted Austin with approval (though he felt that Austin might have overstated the case) and further said:

> [T]here can be little doubt that the time of a Member of Congress can and should be fully consumed in adequately considering the great and difficult questions of substantive policy presented for his decision. If the Office of Legislative Counsel is able, in any substantial degree, to assist the member in the time consuming consideration, the value of the Office, as a governmental instrumentality, will not be effectively disputed.

179. *Id.*

CHAPTER 6

180. As illustrations, the Supreme Court has said, "... we do not consider Congress can ... withdraw from judicial cognizance any matter which, from its nature, is the subject of a suit at the common law, or in equity, or admiralty...." *Murray's Lease v. Hoboken Land & Improvement Co.,* 59 U.S. (18 How.) 272, 284 (1856), cited in Professor Bernard Schwartz' text, ADMINISTRATIVE LAW, at 59 (Boston: Little Brown & Co., 1976). The Court has also refused to enforce a statutory provision authorizing the judiciary to exercise the power to license as a non-judicial function, *Federal Radio Comm. v. General Electric Co.,* 281 U.S. 464, 50 S. Ct. 389, 74 L. Ed. 969 (1930), cited by Professor Louis L. Jaffe in JUDICIAL CONTROL OF ADMINISTRATIVE ACTION at 106 (see Note 111 above); and see *Davis V. Lubbock,* 160 Tex. 38, 326 S.W.2d 699, 714 (1959) (*de novo* judicial review provision of the Texas Urban Renewal statute held unconstitutional as offending the separation of powers provisions of the Texas Constitution since it required independent judicial redetermination of a "pure public policy" question), cited in J. FitzGerald, *The Administrative Law Opinions of Chief Justice Joe R. Greenhill,* 8 Thurgood Marshall L. REV. (Texas Southern University) 265 et seq. (1983).

181. R. Kirk & J. McClellan, THE POLITICAL PRINCIPLES OF ROBERT A. TAFT, at 104 (New York: Fleet Press, 1967).

182. R. Pound, 2 JURISPRUDENCE 322–23 (St. Paul: West Publishing Co., 1959).

183. FEDERALIST, No. 15.

184. A. Koch, JEFFERSON AND MADISON: THE GREAT COLLABORATION, at 44 (New York: Knopf, 1950).

185. FEDERALIST, No. 37.

Resolution of the House of Delegates, American Bar Association, August 13, 1973

Resolved:

[T]hat the President designate the Department of Justice to review and report to the Office of Management and Budget and to the originating agency within a reasonable period of time with respect to each legislative proposal initiated or reported on by the executive branch, an instrumentality thereof, or an independent administrative tribunal or independent regulatory board or commission (hereinafter 'administrative agency') whether such proposal sufficiently sets forth legislative policies and standards for exercise of the powers, functions, and duties proposed to be delegated by the Congress to the administrtive agency. As used herein, the term 'administrative agency' shall not include the Administrative Conference of the United States, the Department of the Treasury, or the Internal Revenue Service. Such report should be in writing and transmitted to the Congress with the legislative proposal of the administrative agency and the opinion of the counsel for the administrative agency on the same matter. No legislative proposal or report on a bill should be submitted to the Congress by an administrative agency until such a Department of Justice report has been issued. Circular No. A-19 of the Office of Management and Budget should be amended appropriately to effectuate this recommendation.

... that Congress or each house thereof designate a legislative committee, office, staff, or consultant to review, draft, and report with respect to whether a legislative proposal delegating discretionary powers to an administrative agency, sufficiently sets forth legislative policies and standards for the exercise of the powers, functions, and duties proposed to be delegated by the Congress. The legal report should be in writing and, together with the opinions transmitted from the Department of Justice and administrative agency counsel, should be incorporated by each committee report recommending a bill for consideration and vote by the members of the Senate or House, and omission to include such reports and opinions may subject the consideration of the bill to a point of order upon request of a member. . . . August 13, 1973 (59 A.B.A.J. 1131, 1142 [1973]).

*Appendix II**
Review of Proposed Legislative Delegations in Europe and Britain

Consultations were held with judges, scholars, government officials, and former officials in a number of European countries (Great Britain, France, Switzerland, West Germany, Italy, Greece, Austria, Belgium, Portugal, and Spain). Available constitutional and other materials were examined, and reports were written and submitted for comment. The subjects of inquiry: whether such statutory delegations of legislative power were common and acceptable, and what means existed to avoid enactment of standardless grants of authority. The general answers were that the problem was present and needed redressing, and in several instances

*Grateful acknowledgment is made of consultations held with the following persons (including persons in Germany, the procedure of which is referred to only in Chapter 6): *Austria*: Dr. Wilhelm F. Czerny, Director of Parliament; Dr. Klaus Berchtold, Constitutional Service Office, Verfassungsdienst des Bundeskanzleramts; Dr. Gunther Winkler, Juridische Fakultat, Universitat Wien. *Belgium*: Dean J. DeMeyer, Dean of the Faculty of Law, Catholic University of Louvain; Professor Louis Paul Suetens, Director of the Institute for Administrative Law, Catholic University of Louvain; J. Mertens de Wilmars, Justice of the Court of Justice of the European Communities, Belgium; Erik Suy, Member of the Cabinet of the Minister of Foreign Affairs. *France*: M. Ducamin, Secretary-General, Conseil d'Etat; M. Francois Goguel, Conseil Constitutionnel of France; M. Luchaire, President de l'Université Paris I; Nicole Questiaux, Counsel, Conseil d'Etat; Michel Morisot, Maitre des Requétes (Master of Requests), Conseil d'Etat. *Germany*: Hon. Fabian von Schlabrendorff, Associate Justice, Bundesverfassungsericht; Dr. Wolfgang Heyde, Ministerialrat, Federal Ministry of Justice; Dr. Johann-Friedrich Staats, Regierungsdirektor, Federal Ministry of Justice; Professor Dr. Quaritsch, Director, Wissenschaftlicher Dienst des Deutschen Bundestages; Dr. Kremer, Wissenschaftlicher Dienst des Deutschen Bundestages; Dr. von Loewenish, Ministry of Interior; Dr. Meinhard Hilf, Max-Planck-Institut fuer Auslandisches Offentliches Recht und Volkerrecht; Dr. Ewald Metzler, M.C.L., University of Frankfurt; the late Dr. Heinrich Kronstein, Director of Trade Regulation, University of Frankfurt, and Professor of Law, Georgetown University, Washington, D.C, U.S.A.; Dr. Werner F. Ebke, Visiting Associate Professor of Law, Southern Methodist University, Dallas, Texas, U.S.A. *Switzerland*: Dr. Thomas Fleiner-Gerster, Professor an der juristischen Fakultat, Decanat de la Faculte de Droit et des Sciences Economiques et Sociales, Univrsite de Fribourg; Thomas Cottier, Dr. iur, LL.M., Fursprecher, Universitat Bern; Dr. Christopher Lanz, LL.M., Sekretariat der Bundesversammiung, Bern. *United Kingdom*: Sir Kenneth Roberts-Wray, G.C.M.G., Q.C., D.C.L., retired Chief Legal Adviser of the Commonwealth Relations Office and the Colonial Office; H.W.R. Wade, Q.C., L.L.D., D.C.L., Professor of Law, University of Oxford; A.B. Lyons, Editor of Statutory Instruments; Professor D.C. Holland, M.A., Law Faculty, University College, University of London.

that constructive action had been taken to accomplish this result. Brief reference is made to some of the foreign procedures below, with emphasis upon the method of preenactment review of statutes.

AUSTRIA

The Federation of Austrian States is a federal state, not a federation of sovereign states. The Constitutional Court has stated that all relevant provisions must be contained in a statute dealing with public administration in view of the provision of Article 18 (2) of the Constitution that ordinances (regulations) of administrative authorities must be issued '... on the basis of the laws. ...'' A more liberal construction since 1923 has not occasioned a retreat from the principle.

Most of the laws are prepared by the administration and proposed by the government. Each department has its own staff for drafting proposals to the Parliament. The Parliament itself is not staffed well, and usually it makes only minor changes in the administration draft of a bill; however, the small size of the staff available for this kind of work in Parliament is only one part of the problem. Another part is the party problem. Since the Chancellor is not only the chief executive officer, but also the head of the party in the majority in the National Council (one of the two houses of Parliament), there is a strong tendency to accept in the Parliament what is sent in the way of bills from the executive.

In Austria, as (theoretically) contrasted with the United States, the executive can introduce bills into the Parliament. However, before a minister can introduce a bill, he must first send it to the Constitutional Service Office. This office, which is attached to the Chancellor, has as its main function the review of the drafting of bills to determine that they do not present constitutional questions. Its powers are simply advisory, but the advice is given to the Chancellor. Should he say no to the bill as a result of an unfavorable report, the bill will no longer be sent to the Parliament since all the ministers must be in accord on legislation before it can be introduced and the Chancellor is a part of the ministry.

The office is a section of the Chancery and is staffed by ten professional jurists. The review of drafts of bills is a principal but not the only duty and responsibility that this office has. Its staff is competent for all questions relating to constitutionality of bills and other matters, especially questions of amending the constitution. It has the responsibility of approving all drafts of bills of various ministers in light of the constitution and giving its written opinion, which though not legally binding is effectively binding. The office also intervenes in the Constitutional Court on the constitutionality of a law or decree.

Bills directed to the Office from a Minister are accompanied by explanatory memoranda to which the office can turn if the bill as drafted contains language that is too vague. In addition to using supporting explanations from such memoranda in redrafting bills, the office also negotiates with the minister's office to attempt to overcome the constitutional question or to improve the language of the bill. The copy of the office opinion is sometimes used by the Chancellor in reading to the Parliament the view of the office on a bill pending. The chief of the office is also often called to give his opinion to the committees of the National Council on amendments to bills. However, it does appear that after the office returns the bill to a minister for redrafting, or to send its comments to the minister, the draft as revised is not returned to the office for review so that there is no assurance that the bill as it is finally sent to the Parliment after a redrafting process is satisfactory to these experts.

BELGIUM

A new constitution was adopted December 24, 1970. It provides for a constitutional and parliamentary monarchy with a system of separation of powers. The executive authority is vested in the King, who appoints the ministers who countersign his acts; legislative authority is exercised collectively by the King, the House of Representatives, and the Senate, except for cultural matters; and the judiciary authority is exercised by the courts and tribunals. The authoritative interpretation of laws is solely the prerogative of the legislative authority.

Eighty percent of the effective bills are introduced by the executive, which compares fairly closely with the United States. In Belgium, somewhat similar to the case of France, a legislative panel of the Supreme Administrtive Court examines all bills introduced into the House of Representatives or the Senate by the Executive. (Earlier it was confined to giving advice on laws and regulations.) It is required that executive bills be so processed. The legislative panel of the Supreme Administrative Court review the bills to determine whether they are constitutional and whether their content is validly drawn. The decision on the part of the legislative panel is not binding on the executive.

The administrative court is entitled the Council of State. as in France, and its functions appear quite similar. Theoretically it is in the executive branch, but in fact it is quite independent. Its opinions on the drafts of bills originating with the executive branch are not binding on the Parliament.

In the beginning, the legislative section of the Council or State concentrated on the language of a bill, that is to say, on the manner of its drafting. However, as time went on the legislative section became concerned more and more about questions of legality and constitutionality. A government bill when it reaches the legislative section is accompanied by a memoir that explains the substance of the bill. In connection with their review the legislative panel personnel draft and redraft the bills, and they hear witnesses from the executive department.

The Council of State consists of eighteen councillors, appointed for life, who work on a full-time basis, six of them in the legislative section and twelve in the administrtive section. There are also ten assessors (consultants) who assist part-time. The consultants are prominent attorneys, including professors of law, who are specialists in constitutional law and other relevant areas of the law. They meet with the panel and review the language and draft as called upon. In addition, forty auditors are assigned to either administrative or legislative section work or to both.

Within the Council of State the bills are considered after receiving a report from one of the auditors for the Council. If a special problem arises on reading the report the Council can ask the auditor to have a government official appear, but this would be unusual. There is a strong feeling in the Council of State, which is apparently shared in other countries by the special review staffs—those within either the executive, legislative, or judicial departments whose sole function is to examine for validity pending government bills—that a special competence and talent and training is required for this work that the normal government lawyer would not possess. Legislative drafting is of course an art in itself. When this is combined with the need for being familiar with constitutional principles and decisions, and with the hosts of other statutes that may be affected by the passage of the bill being examined, it becomes clear that a highly technical and professional type of specialty is involved.

When the Council of State has examined the bill, it draws to the attention of the government any questions it may have, such as extreme vagueness of language or statutory ambiguities. It applies in the main three tests. One is whether personal and property rights are being arbitrarily destroyed or damaged. Another is whether the statutory language is so vague it bestows a breadth of discretion that could be too arbitrarily exercised or unequally applied, causing discrimination. Third, a vague law is questioned under separation of powers doctrine, namely, does the bill proposed convey a legislative power to the executive.

Some government ministers look on the legislative review function of the Council of State as useful, others as unduly complicating their administration of policy. In the end, the review work done is quite beneficial to the drafting of statutory law, except that the government can circumvent the Council in case of urgency. For quite a considerable number of bills, urgency is invoked.

The phrase "in the public interest" would be considered by the panel as too vague and too limitless in the discretionary power conferred. As to this kind of language, it is the custom of the panel to ask for revision and precision. This is not to say that Belgium does not have broad legislative standards in its laws. It does, but it attempts to see that they are not unnecessarily broad.

FRANCE

Under the French constitution of 1958, organic laws are those enacted by Parliament that develop in detail and amplify certain specific subjects identified in the constitution such as civil rights, nationality, the general organization of national defense, determination of crimes and misdemeanors and their penalties, or the electoral system. Organic laws must set forth the rules applicable to such laws, thus requiring some detail to be enacted by Parliament.

All other laws are defined as regulatory. In enacting a regulatory law, Parliament need only set forth the fundamental principles, leaving the government much more breadth of action in issuing decrees under regulatory laws—though the government's power to issue decrees in clarification of the rules set forth by Parliament in organic laws is also wide. Government decrees may only be legislated by the President after consultation with the Council of State, that is, in a way similar to the consultation with this administrative court on government bills to be submitted to parliament, mentioned below.

Pre-enactment Review in the Government

The Council of State (Conseil d'Etat) gives nonbinding advice to the government related to every aspect of the law and constitution on each government bill that Parliament is being requested to enact into law. In determining whether to approve a proposed bill, the vital consideration confronting the Council of State, as related to the issue under discussion, would be whether such questions of form and vagueness exist that proper execution of the proposed bill cannot take place. Such review by the Coucil of State has resulted in more definiteness of language in such bills through the suggestion of the Council of State or through joint consultation efforts with the government. The Council of State firmly believes in the value of sharpening a bill so that vagueness is removed.

The Council of State is the supreme court of France concerning administrative disputes. Litigation against the government occupies most of its time. The same personnel in the Council of State act both in the advisory opinion function and on litigated cases. However, it is estimated that if all of the time given by the various members of the staff of the Council of State is considered, approximately fifty full-time jobs in the higher grade of French civil service are involved in the advisory role.

Pre-enactment Review in Parliament

The Constitutional Council, third court in the judiciary, is required by Article 61 of the French Constitution to rule upon the constitutionality of organic laws *before their promulgation*, and upon regulations of the parliamentary assemblies before they come into application. At the request of the President, the Premier, or the President of one of the other Assembly (and only these four), the Constitutional Council can review and approve or disapprove other laws in advance of their promulgation. Its decisions are not appealable (Article 62).

SWITZERLAND

The Confederation of Swiss States dates from the adoption of a constitution in 1848, which was totally revised in 1874 and has undergone more than a hundred amendments since 1874. By constitutional provision the several independent cantons transferred some power to the confederation and retained others.

The Swiss federal parliament, called the Federal Assembly, consists of two chambers: the National Council and the Council of States. Article

71 of the constitution vests the "supreme power" of the confederation in the Federal Assembly, subject to the rights of the people and the cantons (Articles 89, 89 *bis*, 123). The cantons administer most of the laws, ordinances, and regulations, national as well as cantonal. Thus a federal statute concerning water pollution authorizes the cantons to excercise its provisions, which they do through enactment and administration of cantonal acts.

The Federal Assembly elects the Federal Council (the executive), and Supreme Court (Federal Tribunal). The government is the Federal Council, a cabinet of seven members elected by the United Federal Assembly for four years. The Supreme Court's function as a constitutional tribunal is limited to review of cantonal statutes, interstate compacts and interstate ordinances; it does not extend to federal statutes. The actual exception is when federal statutes directly bear upon cantonal statutes and local ordinances in litigation decided by the cantonal courts in cases subsequently appealed to the Federal Tribunal.

In a long series of precedents, when reviewing cantonal statutes and in decisions on appeals, the Federal Tribunal worked out the rule that delegation is permissible, when not explicitly forbidden by the cantonal constitution, if it is restricted to specific issues and if the statute itself provides the basic content and purpose of the regulation.

Pre-enactment Review

The members of Parliament are part-time representatives, and the staff of the secretariat of the Federal Assembly has been very limited until recently. The Federal Council is required by the law regulating its relations with the Federal Assembly to include in every report to the Federal Assembly proposing a new statute or the amendment of an existing one a special chapter dealing with the constitutionality of its proposals. This obligation has just been amended: both houses have approved a provision according to which the Federal Council will also have to motivate explicitly every proposed statutory delegation.

It is interesting to observe that there now exists a special service within the Federal Justice Department particularly dealing with pre-enactment control of federal legislation. The particular duty of the Principal Division of Legislation, a branch of the Federal Office of Justice, is to screen legislative drafts (proposed statutes, ordinances, regulations, and respective amendments) and report on their consistence and constitutionality and, with respect to ordinances, on their legality. All drafts are scrutinized twice, first considering the original draft, and second considering the final draft before promulgation and, with respect to statute projects, before they go to Parliament. One of the central issues in this quasi-judicial, albeit consultative, process is the question of delegation. The Service widely applies the standards as developed by the Federal Tribunal mentioned above. By the creation of this Principal Division of Legislation a useful attempt was made to avoid unreasonable delegation. In the view of one observer it might be helpful in the future to enlarge the Service and make it available to Parliament and its commissions, directly.

UNITED KINGDOM

There is no written constitution, and the supremacy of Parliament is established. For these reasons and because of the lack of a separtion of powers doctrine, there is nothing unconstitutional or illegal in Parliament's delegating all of the lawmaking power to the Crown on any given subject, though other things and chiefly poilitical reality stand in the way of its doing so. The executive, while answerable to Parliament, is realistically, as is Parliament, a separate body and institution with separate and different functions. The ministers are the administrators of the government. Broad power has been delegated to administrators. S.A. de Smith in his *Judicial Review of Administrative Action* (fourth ed., edited by J.M. Evans [1980]) states:

> The Government commands the lion's share of parliamentary time. Of the Public Bills that reach the Statute book, the vast majority are Government Bills. . . . Bills are subject to amendment at the committee and report stages, but they hardly ever go to select committees (which have inquisitorial powers). (p. 346)

When any department wishes a bill to be introduced into Parliament and its introduction has been approved by the appropriate political committee, the department sends instruction to Parliamentary Counsel, and it is his office that drafts the bill. The Office of Parliamentary Counsel is a body of skilled government lawyers and drafters who are civil servants of the Parliament but compensated by the Treasury Department. The office is independent of any minister and is probably an arm of Parliament according to British legal opinion. The First Parliamentary Counsel is in charge of the office. That offical is one of the most imporatnt and most highly paid lawyers in the government service. His office drafts bills only on the instruction of a government minister.

The drafter could raise a question regarding undue breadth of language but must take his instruction from the minister responsible for the subject. That applies to all government bills. Parliamentary Counsel are not necessarily involved, though they often assist, in drafting a bill introduced by a Private Member. There are comparatively few of these bills, the situation being roughly comparable with that in Austria. There are also "Private Bills," that is, bills that apply only to particular districts, organizations, or persons. They are promoted by the people concerned, and it is doubtful if Parliamentary Counsel are ever concerned in the drafting of such bills.

Post-enactment Review

Under the Statutory Instruments Act of 1946, "statutory instruments" (the term for rules that adminstrative agencies are authorized by the statutes to make) were defined. Every statute delegating rulemaking power must provide expressly that the minister shall make rules "by statutory instrument" unless it is intended that the act shall not apply. The definition of "statutory instruments" includes the rules made by such instruments and Orders in Council (exercises of rulemaking power of any particular minister).[1]

Most such rules and orders in council are required by the agency statute to be laid before Parliament:[2] for example, the Housing Act must state which orders are to considered statutory instruments; others are not so considered. The agency statute provides just what the laying effect shall be. In broad outline, the basic forms follow.[3] The statute may

---

1. Bernard Schwartz and H.W. Wade, *Legal Control of Government,* (1972), pp. 99–100.

2. Id., p. 100.

3. A.B. Lyons, the editor of *Statutory Instruments,* outlines the forms: 1. Laying in draft (a) for affirmative resolution (approval); (b) for negative resolution; (c) without further proceedings. 2. Laying after making (a) for affirmative resolution, (i) the instrument does not come into operaton, (ii) the instrument ceases to operate after a specified period (usually twenty-eight days) unless approved by then; (b) for negative resolution, the instrument has immediate effect but is subject to annulment (this is the most usual form of control, and the actual annulling is by orders in council, but such orders are infrequent); (c) without further proceedings.

provide that the rule is effective unless annulled by a vote of either House, within a given number of days ("laying" being the British method of requiring by statute that administrative rules be filed with Parliment a specified period of time for consideration, rejection or annulment). This is the common form of laying provision: a member may criticize a filed rule and move its annulment within forty days.[4] The less common method is when the agency statute provides that the laid rule shall not be effective unless and until approved by parliamentary resolution.[5]

Scrutiny committees in each House examine rules required to be laid. The House of Lords committee examines only the orders that require affirmative resolution; the House of Commons Select Committee on Statutory Instruments examines all filed rules (as well as draft rules that are laid), and may request the appearance of the minister or his representative if it has a question, such as whether the instrument makes some unusual or unexpected use of the powers conferred by the statue under which it is made; imposes a charge on the public revenue or requires payment to be made by the subject to a government department or other authority; or is retrospective in its application, or has been delayed in publication or laying, or is unclear, and so forth. In practice if members of the House of Commons Statutory Instruments Committee have questions they raise them in letters to the departments which are written by the clerk to the committee. If a representative of the department appears personally he can be and is questioned by any member of the committee. The committee meets fortnightly. It reports to the whole House, drawing attention to the statutory instrument concerned on any of the grounds specified in the committee's terms of reference.

Usually the Parliament has no power to amend the filed rule, but must consider it upon a "take it or leave it" basis. The rule can be annulled by action under this procedure, or approved, within the period established by the Statutory Instruments Act: forty (or twenty-eight) days. Under the negative resolution procedure, the instrument is effective on making and remains effective unless and until it is annuled.[6]

---

4. Schwartz and Wade, *Legal Control of Government*, p. 101.

5. Id.

6. Consultations with Sir Kenneth Roberts-Wray, retired Chief Legal Officer, British Colonial Office; A.B. Lyons, Editor of Statutory Instruments; see also The Hansard Society Symposium (1949), 99–100; H.W.R. Wade, Administrative Law [of Britain] 3rd ed. (1971), 331–337.

SUMMARY

Greater attention is paid in Europe and Britain to the drafting of laws in a manner calulated to retain the political (policy decision) power and function in the legislature. This may be due in part to the fact that most European countries are governed by the code system; perhaps it is in part due to the fact that they have been in existence much longer and have not grown so rapidly. However, in Europe also there is a sharp awareness of the problem discussed. In several of these countries, unlike the United States, the ministers are also members of Parliament, hence the administrative department heads are subject to regular questioning by the legislative department concerning the legality and wisdom of their actions during debates in the legislative halls and during Question periods, such as those continuously scheduled in England.

Some countries but not all, notably not Britain, put the problem in a separation of powers context, as well as their administrators' lack of ability to develop and promulgate broad legislative concepts. All believe that the complexities of government require bestowal upon the executive of considerable administrative discretion and flexibility. The laying system that Britain has employed for many years under Statutory Instruments acts is not a possibility for adoption in the United States due to a Supreme Court decision, cited in the text, that held that the constitutional veto authority of the president could not be thus avoided. Moreover, it would be, if available, at most a band-aid remedy to a grave separation of powers difficulty: occasional congressional rejection of a single regulation of a federal adminsitrative agency does little to clothe an overbroad statutory delegation with definiteness.

INDEX

ABOUT THE AUTHOR

Professor FitzGerald began teaching as a professor of law at Southern Methodist University in 1961, where he taught primarily Administrative Law, Local Government Law and Federal Agency Practice. He also served as visiting professor of law at Hastings College of Law, University of Southern California Law Center, and Boston College Law School. Previous to 1961 he was General Counsel (1958-61) and chief of the Review Staff (1954-58) of the Federal Communications Commission and Legal Consultant to the Minority Staff of the Banking and Currency Committee of the House of Representatives (1961). He has held various legal postions with the government housing agencies, as well as having been in 1948-49 General Counsel of the Housing Authority of the County of Los Angeles. He is author of numerous law review articles and bar reports dealing with the statutory powers and procedures of Federal and local adminstrative agencies, municipal law and constitutional separation of powers issues.

For a number of years he was the Chairman of the Separation of Powers Committee of the American Bar Association's Administrative Law Section and a member of the Council, and was Consultant (1978-81) to the Administrative Conference of the United States (with respect to the feasibility of requiring Federal Administrative agencies to adopt uniform rules of adjudicatory procedure). Born in Seattle, and a graduate of the University of Washington and its law school, he holds graduate degrees from Harvard Law School and Georgetown Law Center. He is a member of the Bars of Washington, California and Texas, having engaged in the private practice of law in Seattle, Los Angeles and presently in Dallas where he and his wife and two of their four sons reside.